Apprenticeship Workbook

Children's Care, Learning and Development

Chris Pritchard

www.harcourt.co.uk
✓ Free online support
✓ Useful weblinks
✓ 24 hour online ordering

01865 888118

Heinemann
From Harcourt

Heinemann Educational Publishers
Halley Court, Jordan Hill, Oxford OX2 8EJ
Part of Harcourt Education

Heinemann is the registered trademark of Harcourt Limited

First published 2007

10 09 08 07 06
10 9 8 7 6 5 4 3 2 1

British Library Cataloguing in Publication Data is available from the British Library on request.

13-digit ISBN: 978 0 435449 13 1

In-house team
Publisher: Beth Howard
Managing Editor: Faye Cheeseman
Design: Georgia Bushell
Picture Research: Chrissie Martin
Production: Jamie Copping

Copyedited by Helen Maxey
Designed by Kamae Design, Oxford
Typeset by Tek-Art, Croydon, Surrey
Original illustrations © Harcourt Education Limited, 2006
Illustrated by Alasdair Bright & Tek-Art
Cover design by Kamae Design, Oxford
Printed in China by CTPS
Cover photo: © Alamy

Websites: Please note that the examples of websites suggested in this book were up to date at the time of writing. It is essential for tutors to preview each site before using it to ensure that the URL is still accurate and the content is appropriate. We suggest that tutors bookmark useful sites and consider enabling students to access them through the school or college intranet.

Name of apprentice: ______________________________

Placement: ______________________________

Start date: ______________________________

Acknowledgements

The author and publisher would like to thank the following individuals and organisations for permission to reproduce photographs:

Alamy Images/Bubbles Photolibrary p**7**; Alamy Images/Carl Payne p**123**; Alamy Images/Dan Atkin p**62**; Alamy Images/Photofusion Picture Library p**125**; Alamy Images/Sally and Richard Greenhill p**118**; Alamy Images/ Visions of America, LLC p**49**; Bubbles pp**2**(top), **124**; Corbis p**126**; Cristina Fumi/Alamy p**90**; Eyewire pp**47**, **92**, **157**; Fotolibra/Bernard Howden p**108**; Getty Images/Image Bank p**50**; Getty Images/PhotoDisc pp**viii**, **146**(top); Getty Images/Taxi p**iii**; Harcourt Education Ltd/Gareth Boden pp**10**, **30**(top); Harcourt Education Ltd/Jules Selmes pp **vii**, **2**(bottom), **8**, **15**, **23**, **28**(top and bottom), **30**(bottom), **32**, **38**, **45**, **46**, **52**, **53**, **65**, **71**, **73**, **74**, **76**, **83**, **84**(top and bottom), **86**, **87**, **88**, **89**, **94**, **95**, **97**, **98**, **99**, **101**, **102**, **106**, **109**, **110**, **112**, **122**, **127**, **129**, **130**, **132**, **133**, **136**, **137**, **141**, **143**, **144**, **145**, **148**, **149**, **151**, **155**, **156**; Harcourt Education Ltd/Peter Morris p**146**(bottom); Harcourt Education Ltd/Tudor Photography pp**9**, **24**, **29**, **70**, **103**, **135**, **138**; MedioImages p**21**; Rubberball Productions p**140**.

Every effort has been made to contact copyright holders of material reproduced in this book. Any omissions will be rectified in subsequent printings if notice is given to the publishers.

Contents

Introduction to the components of the framework for the apprenticeship in Children's Care, Learning and Development

Charts and diagrams for candidates to fill out and add to their portfolio are also available to download **for free** from www.heinemann.co.uk/vocational. Click on *Childcare* on the subject list, then *Free Resources* under the Resource Centre at the top right of the screen.

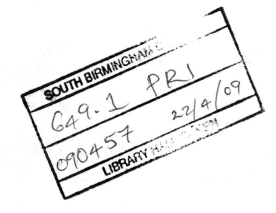

Guide to the workbook

Introduction

This workbook has been written primarily for you, 'the apprentice', as an holistic assessment plan integrating the six components of the apprenticeship framework. The book has been broken down into chapters with a specific topic area in each.

Within the workbook you will find a variety of tasks, assignments and activities to be made up and completed by yourself for the benefit of the children.

The workbook is a personal book, exclusively for your own use. It is addressed to you. You can write in it, putting in your target dates and any other comments you find helpful.

There are occasions when performance criteria are evidenced more than once. Don't worry – this is good practice for you. Activities can be practised as often as time will allow but you are advised to ask a colleague for feedback.

Hints & Tips

Remember to read through the whole chapter before you begin any of its tasks.

Always use an action plan. This helps to organise you and reminds you of all the mini-tasks you must carry out.

When you feel competent and confident, then it is time to ask your assessor to observe you. **Remember**: always plan your observation time with your assessor in advance.

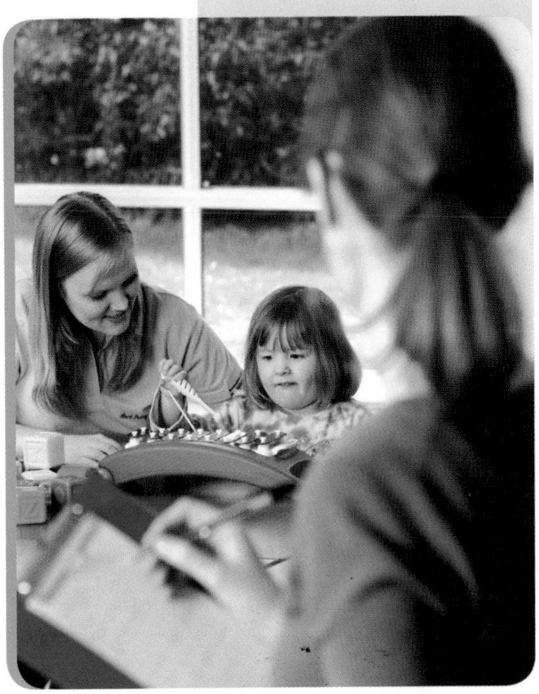

After a direct observation, your assessor will ask you questions related to your performance which will give you the opportunity to demonstrate your knowledge, understanding and skills.

This will cover some of the knowledge evidence of the NVQ (National Vocational Qualification) units.

You must gather evidence for your portfolio using one or more of the evidence-gathering methods suggested in the workbook, or they can be found in the units of the NOS (National Occupational Standards).

Your portfolio should contain your child observations, assessor observations, expert witness testimonies, work products and all other evidence gathered for the five components of the apprenticeship framework. (For more information about the framework, see the qualifications section beginning on page 1.)

Your assessor will help you to file the evidence in the order required by the Assessment Centre.

The work must be of your own making and be presented to your assessor/tutor by the appointed time.

Each piece of work must be named, dated and signed by you to authenticate the work as your own. Your assessor will initial the work when he or she has assessed it.

Note to the assessor

This workbook is a tool to help the apprentice but in no way can it replace the experience, value and guidance of the efficient assessor.

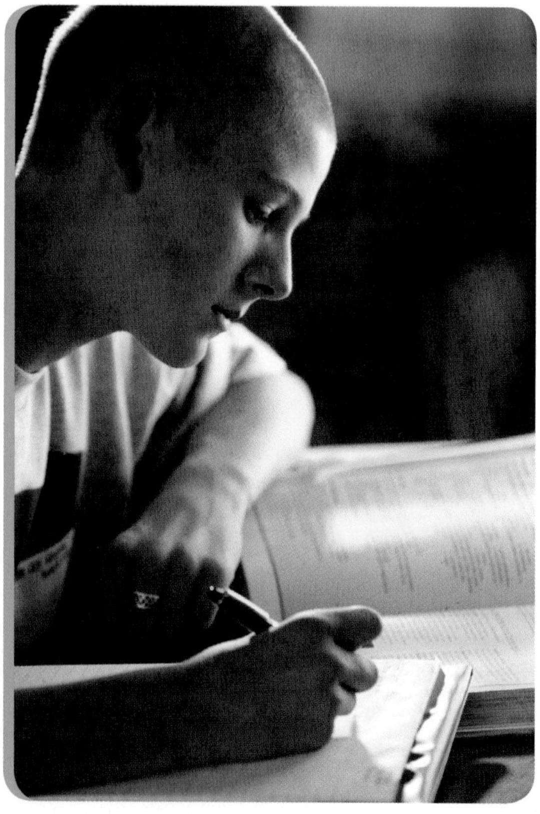

It can be used as a base for designing specific action or assessment plans, should further interpretation be needed.

The apprentice can work alone in parts of this book – for example, questions, research, tasks (which can be an advantage as it can shorten the time allocated on the scheme) – but it cannot replace the assessor (or expert witness), who must observe some part of each element of the NVQ.

Templates for assignments can be photocopied from this handbook or downloaded free from the Heinemann website.

Symbols in the workbook

Hints and tips

You will find tips and hints to help you gather your evidence wherever you see this owl symbol.

EGM boxes

EGM stands for 'evidence gathering method'. You can use different methods to get the evidence you need, and you will find suggestions as to which method to use highlighted in the margin (as shown).

EGM Direct Observation

Assessor check

The little flags are to remind you that your assessor will be checking your understanding of the knowledge evidence and may ask you questions about your performance.

Useful acronyms and terms

ALI	Adult Learning Inspectorate
AON	Application of Number
C&G	City and Guilds
CC	Common Core
CCLD	Children's Care, Learning and Development
Com	Communication
CWDC	Children's Workforce Development Council
DfES	Department for Education and Skills
ECM	Every Child Matters
EGM	Evidence Gathering Method
ERR	Employment Rights and Responsibilities
H&S	Health and Safety
his/her	*Read*: his or her
ICT	Information Communication Technology
IOL	Improving Own Learning
ITP	Individual Training Plan
K.Skill	Key Skill
KU	Knowledge and Understanding
Line Manager	*Read*: Room Leader, Key Worker, Senior Childcare practitioner, Nursery Nurse Group Leader
Manager	*Read*: Officer in Charge, Supervisor, Person in Charge
NDCS	National Day Care Standards
NOS	National Occupational Standards

NQF	National Qualification Framework
NVQ	National Vocational Qualification
Ofsted	Office for Standards in Education
parent/ guardian	*Read*: parent or guardian
PC	Performance Criteria
PS	Problem solving
s/he	*Read*: she or he
TC	Technical Certificate
WWO	Working With Others

Guide to page layout

Explanation of page set-up				
The second column on the right-hand side of the page has been set up to guide you to the related set of standards that you must use for the activity described in the main column on the left-hand side of the page.				
The purple bars tell you that you are to use the National Vocational Qualification (NVQ) standards and contain the following information:	**NVQ**	**203**	**2**	**4**
• the NVQ unit • the NVQ element and performance criteria number.				
The yellow bars tell you that you are to use the Technical Certificate standards and contain the following information:	**T.Cert**	**003**	**A**	**ii**
• the relevant Technical Certificate • the task letter of the Technical Certificate assignment • the number of the task letter of the Technical Certificate assignment.				
The red bars tell you that you are to use the relevant Key Skill and contain information about the Key Skill and the related element.	**K.Skill**	**C1**	**1**	**1**

Apprenticeship qualifications

Introduction to Level 2 apprenticeship

An apprenticeship is the current way for young people and adults to learn and train whilst in a childcare work setting.

Learning for young people

You can study for the apprenticeship at any age between 16 and 24 years. You need to be based as a practitioner employed (or working without pay if under 18 years) in a childcare setting.

16–24 yrs

Apprenticeships are an integrated, holistic way of learning.

The apprenticeship framework is produced by the Sector Skills Council and approved by the Apprenticeship Approvals Group.

SSC – Children's Workforce Development Council

The apprenticeship for young people wanting to work with children is called the Apprenticeship in Children's Care, Learning and Development.

The framework is made up of:

- NVQ Level 2 in Children's Care, Learning and Development (CCLD)
- Certificate in Children's Care, Learning and Development (Technical Certificate)
- Application of Number Key Skill at Level 1
- Communication Key Skill at Level 1
- Employment Responsibilities and Rights (ERR) Unit
- 12-hour Paediatric First Aid

NVQ in CCLD

CERT in CCLD

K.Skill – AON

K.Skill – Com

ERR

First Aid

Let's start by looking at the different components of the Apprenticeship Framework.

National Vocational Qualifications (NVQs) are National Occupational Standards (NOS).

NVQs

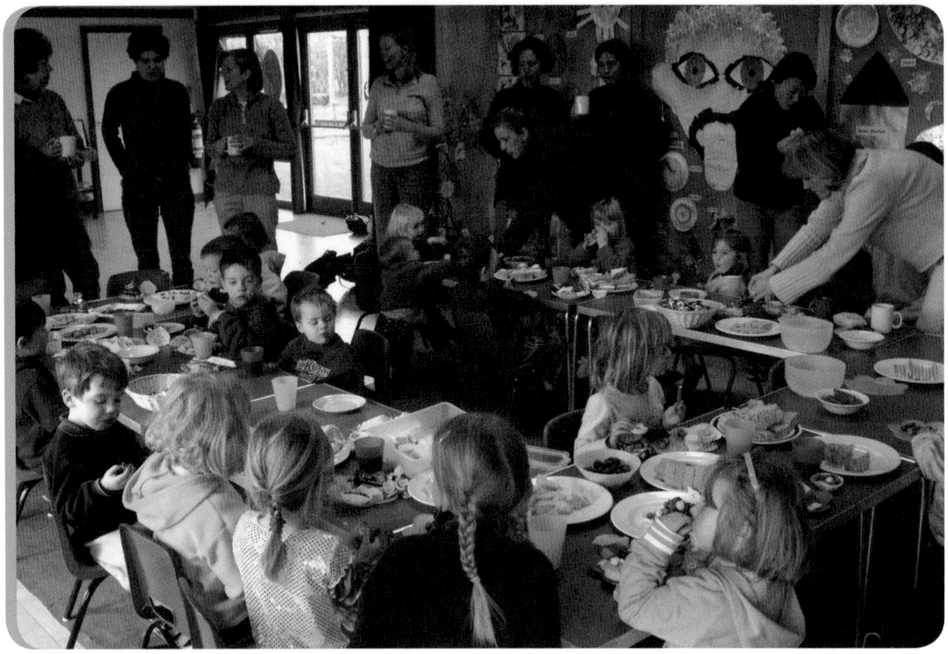

The National Occupational Standards are statements of the skills, knowledge and competence required of a worker in a childcare setting.

NOS

Competence in the Children's Care, Learning and Development (CCLD) NVQ is shown by your skills in the workplace and your knowledge evidence about work with children. Skills in the workplace will be shown by your interaction with children, your understanding of their needs and how competently you care for them.

CCLD

The knowledge evidence can be presented in a folder called a portfolio of evidence, or it can be presented electronically by a web portal tracking system. This allows you to record and attach documents via a sophisticated email

Portfolio

system onto your own virtual portfolio, which can only be accessed by you, your assessor and an Internal Verifier.

You can gain the knowledge evidence by personal research, attending off-the-job training with a work-based learning provider or attending college part-time.

Knowledge evidence

With the CCLD NVQ you are expected to have knowledge and understanding of children aged 0–16 years, but you are assessed and observed in the age group with which you have chosen to work.

0–16 years

In the CCLD NOS at Level 2 there are ten NVQ units. To gain your Level 2 NVQ you must complete seven units. Six of the ten units are mandatory; therefore, you choose one optional unit only to complete the qualification. Unit 210 (optional unit) is especially suitable if you are interested in playwork. The units covered in this workbook include all of the mandatory units and the following two optional units:

Level 2 CCLD
6 mandatory and 1 optional unit

- Unit 207: Contribute to the effectiveness of teams
- Unit 208: Support the development of babies and children under three years.

The Structure of NVQs in Children's Care, Learning and Development

A **unit** denotes the function the practitioner is expected to carry out in the workplace.

For example:
CCLD 202
'Help keep children safe'

The **element** identifies one part of the work the practitioner must carry out.

CCLD 202.1
'Prepare and maintain a safe and healthy environment'

The **performance criteria** describe the quality of work that must be carried out.

CCLD 202.1.4
'Deal with waste safely according to the procedures of the setting'

Knowledge and understanding sets out what you, the practitioner, must know to carry out a competent performance.

CCLD 202 K2H20
'Safe storage of hazardous materials and disposal of waste'

You will quickly see that the unit number, 202, remains the same whether referring to the element, performance criteria or knowledge and understanding. This helps to give you, the learner, an easy referencing system – anything that has the prefix number of 202 is about keeping children safe at Level 2.

With knowledge and understanding there is, again, an easy referencing system.

Taking the above example of CCLD 202 K2H20, let's look at the meaning:

CCLD 202 – unit number
K – means knowledge and understanding (KU)
2 – this stands for the unit level (2)
H – this tells you the knowledge is to do with Health and Safety
20 – this is the unique number of knowledge for Health and Safety

CCLD 202 K2H20
'Routine safety checking and maintenance of equipment. Safe storage of hazardous materials and disposal of waste'

We will discuss knowledge and understanding groups later in the workbook.

An NVQ is like a tree:

The tree represents a unit – it has a number and a name.

The branches represent the elements – they all have titles.

The leaves represent performance criteria – these are mini work standards.

The roots represent the knowledge and understanding – underpinning knowledge for a competent performance.

Many trees represent an orchard – several units make a level.

Knowledge and understanding statements

As you work through the apprenticeship framework, you will acquire a lot of knowledge about children. You will start to know and understand their growth and development, the way they play, socialise and communicate. You will understand how and why certain activities help them with their understanding of the complex world around them.

When you have this knowledge and understanding it should show in your performance at work. If the assessor is not able to observe the knowledge and understanding in your practice then she or he will ask you questions. However the questions are worded, they must be written down and recorded with the rest of your evidence. To clarify reasons for practising or setting out specific activities, the assessor may ask you to take part in a professional discussion – again, this is prepared in advance and the discussion recorded or written down.

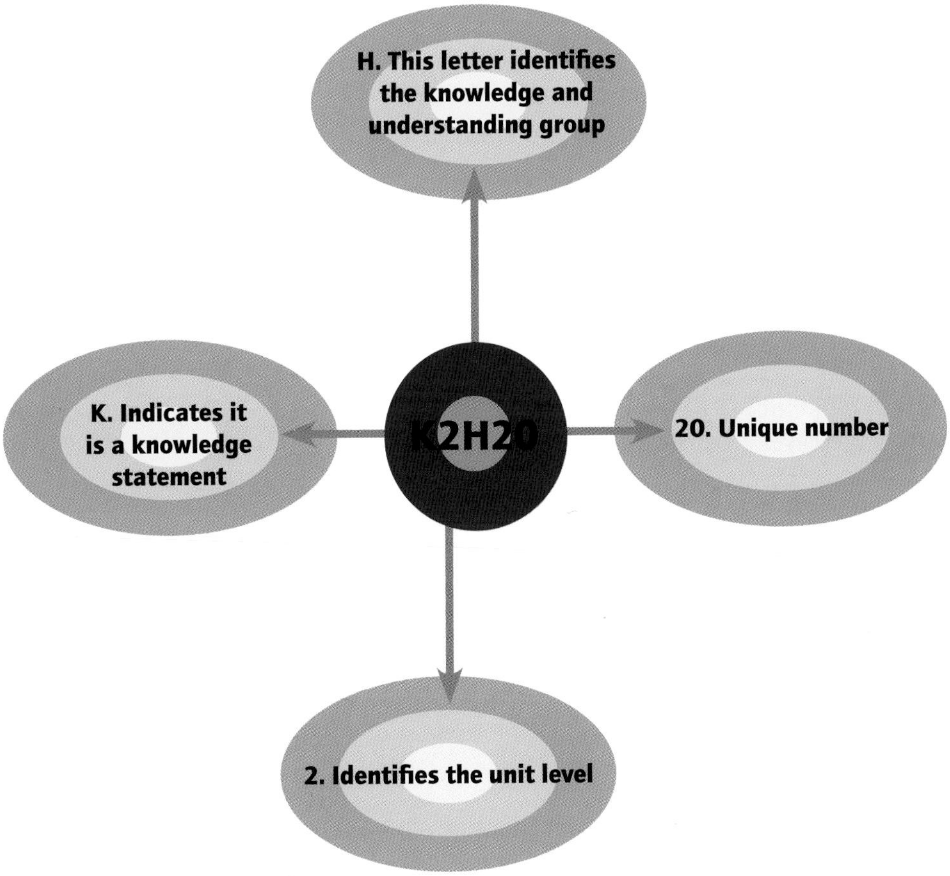

Each unit has a list of knowledge specifications relevant to its elements. Competent performance is dependent upon you demonstrating the knowledge through the activity.

Knowledge statements and identification letter		Common Core reference numbers	
Effective communication and engagement with children, young people, their families and carers	C	1	Effective communication and engagement with children, young people, their families and carers
Child and young person development	D	2	Child and young person development
Health and safety	H		
Multi-agency working	M	5	Multi-agency working
Occupational practice	P		
Safeguarding children and promoting the welfare of the child	S	3	Safeguarding children and promoting the welfare of the child
Supporting transitions	T	4	Supporting transitions
Information	I	6	Sharing information

Technical Certificate in Children's Care, Learning and Development

This workbook is tracked to the City and Guilds Technical Certificate. Technical Certificates are vocational qualifications designed for a particular vocational sector. They can be stand-alone qualifications; which means you can study for the certificate in Children's Care, Learning and Development even if you are not an apprentice. The certificate is on the National Qualifications Framework (NQF).

When Technical Certificates are part of an apprenticeship framework, they deliver the knowledge and understanding that you need to be able to work competently and knowledgeably with children.

The Technical Certificate for Level 2 has four mandatory units. You need to complete all four units to successfully gain the Level 2 certificate.

The grading and marking system for the Technical Certificate is Pass/Refer/Fail:

- **Pass** is when all the tasks within an assignment have been successfully completed.
- **Refer** is when some of the tasks within the unit still need reworking or completing.
- **Fail** is when, after your second attempt, you still have a significant number of tasks that have not been completed to a satisfactory standard.

Key Skills

Included in the framework are Key Skills at Level 1. For the CCLD framework at Level 2 you must gain the following Key Skills:

- Communication at Level 1
- Application of Number at Level 1.

These mandatory Key Skills are described in greater detail below.

It would be sensible to also gain ICT Key Skill at Level 1, as computers are now so much a part of our daily lives. Alternatively, you could combine the three Key Skills in one childcare project and present it as part of your apprenticeship framework.

(A combined Key Skills project of number, literacy and IT is not within the remit of this book. If you wish to pursue this combination, speak to your assessor.)

Altogether, there are six Key Skills at four different levels. At Level 5 there is a single Key Skill which relates to personal development in higher education. The other three Key Skills, called 'wider Key Skills' – Improving Own Learning, Problem Solving and Working with Others – are not mandatory but they are used by practitioners in childcare in their everyday work. It is strongly recommended that you consider gaining accreditation for these wider Key Skills.

Basically, Key Skills are comprised of two parts:

1. Part A is the 'know how to' part, which tells you about the techniques and knowledge required for you to be able to confidently apply the skills in your work.
2. Part B is the 'what you must do' part, where you apply the skills and show your competence. Each bullet point acts like one of the performance criteria, and you must have evidence in your portfolio for each bullet point.

Key skills are required in all aspects of your work, training, learning and social life.

Mandatory Key Skills

The mandatory Key Skills within the CCLD framework are Communication and Application of Number, both at Level 1.

Communication at Level 1

For the Communication qualification you will take part in a discussion, both one-to-one and in a group. You will need to be knowledgeable about your subject and gain a witness testimony from an expert witness.

For example, in your setting you may have a discussion with your key worker (one-to-one) about the behaviour of a child. In your off-the-job training you may have a group discussion, for example, on safety equipment, and gain a testimony from your tutor/assessor.

You will need to read and obtain information from a variety of sources, identifying the main points and reproducing them using new words or images. This should happen automatically as a result of your personal research – just remember to record the sources of your information.

You will probably write reports in your setting about a happening or incident, and you will carry out child observations. Documents should be written in different formats. You will need to proof read and rewrite them. Always take care with the grammatical structure of your sentences and your spelling.

All this work can be used towards your Communication portfolio.

Application of Number at Level 1

Application of Number allows you to demonstrate your skills in the use of number both at work and in your social life. For example, at work you may count the number of children in school today (e.g. there are 26 children in school today). You may be told that half the number of children can go out to play (13 children go out to play).

You read numbers when you read a bus timetable, a pie chart or graph. You may read mathematical information when you want to know the nutritional values of foods, such as figures for a brand of crisps (see opposite).

For Application of Number Level 1 you will need to interpret information from a variety of sources, be able to carry out calculations, explain and record your results and present your findings.

Nutritional information	Per 100 g
Energy	559 kcal
Protein	3.7 g
Carbohydrates	55.3 g
Fat	37.0 g
Sodium	2.8 g
Fibre	1.2 g

Paediatric First Aid

All apprentices on the CCLD Apprenticeship must complete a 12-hour Paediatric First Aid certificate working with children under 12 years.

You can find the criteria for the First Aid scheme of work on the CWDC website (www.surestart.gov.uk) under the title Sure Start First Aid Criteria.

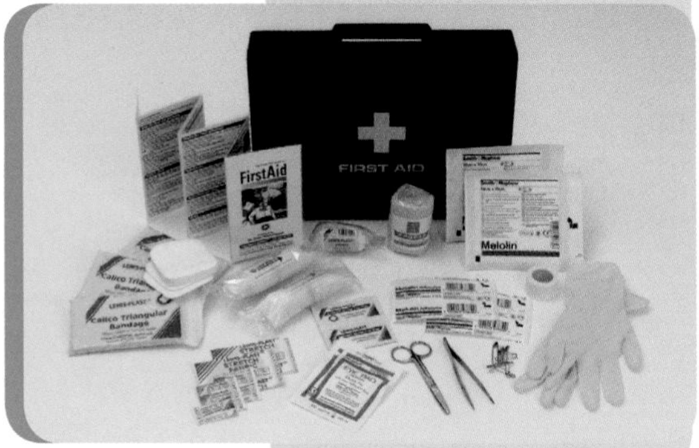

Employment Rights and Responsibilities

The Employment Rights and Responsibilities (ERR) unit is part of the CCLD apprenticeship framework and helps you to understand your rights and responsibilities and those of others at work.

Key elements within the ERR unit are:

- health, safety and security issues
- confidentiality and data protection
- employment rights
- working with children.

This is a unit that can be completed during induction, the early part of your framework or in the Technical Certificate assignments by carrying out a series of activities. It helps you to understand the laws that you must abide by at work and also those that protect you at work.

When you have completed the ERR unit your assessor will sign the Evidence Record form (found at the end of your ERR workbook). This record, together with the NVQ, Technical Certificate, Key Skills and First Aid records, is sent to the Sector Skills Council to gain your CCLD Apprenticeship Framework Certificate.

Food hygiene

Food hygiene is not a mandatory qualification in the apprenticeship framework but it is necessary if you are going to prepare or serve food to the children you work with. The Foundation certificate consists of six hours of coursework and a multiple-choice question paper.

If you are only handling food, for example, serving sandwiches, then you may be able to take a two-hour food hygiene course.

You should seriously consider taking this qualification. Why not discuss it with your assessor or work placement manager?

Quality childcare

Working with children is a very privileged career. People work across a variety of settings including full day care, playgroups, crèches, children's centres, and nursery and primary schools in the private, voluntary and independent sectors. People may also choose to work as a nanny in other people's homes or as childminders in their own home.

In whichever area of childcare you work, there are a set of **principles and values** to which all childcare practitioners must adhere.

Principles and Values

Further criteria that must be considered when working with children is to be found in the following documents:

- 'Common Core of Skills and Knowledge Competence for the Children's Workforce'
- 'Outcomes for Children and Young People' – this is a set of five outcomes identified as being most important to children and young people.

Both of these documents are derived from 'Every Child Matters'.

Common Core

Outcomes for Children

Every Child Matters

Regulated childcare

The government has minimum national standards for childcare. These standards are inspected and regulated by Ofsted. There are 14 National Standards set by the government which apply to all:

- childminders
- full-day care centres
- sessional day care
- crèches
- out-of-school care.

National Day Care Standards

Principles and values

Principles and values form the basis of each unit in the Children's Care, Learning and Development NVQ. You must work within these principles and values, showing that you are committed to the rights of the child and will treat all children accordingly.

Each of us, as individual people, have personal principles – this means our moral rules, our standards, and our sense of duty. When we apply these principles to our work in the childcare sector, we must have the welfare of the child as our first priority and work with the child's parents/guardians, as they know the child best and are the child's first educator.

Think of the principles as accepted standards of behaviour. There are three principles and nine values (see page 11). These principles and values underpin your work with children throughout the CCLD NVQ.

The Technical Certificate has one unit that is dedicated exclusively to principles and values.

Your assessor and your key worker will sign your work to testify that you always work within the principles and values of childcare.

Principles and values for National Occupational Standards in Children's Care, Learning and Development

The principles and values underpin the complete set of standards in their entirety.

Principles

1. The welfare of the child is paramount.
2. Practitioners contribute to children's care, learning and development and this is reflected in every aspect of practice and service provision.
3. Practitioners work with parents and families who are partners in the care, learning and development of their children and are the child's first and most enduring educators.

Values

1. The needs, rights and views of the child are at the centre of all practice and provision.
2. Individuality, difference and diversity are valued and celebrated.
3. Equality of opportunity and anti-discriminatory practice are actively promoted.
4. Children's health and well-being are actively promoted.
5. Children's personal and physical safety is safe guarded, whilst allowing for risk and challenge as appropriate to the capabilities of the child.
6. Self-esteem, resilience and a positive self-image are recognised as essential to every child's development.
7. Confidentiality and agreements about confidential information are respected as appropriate unless a child's protection and well-being are at stake.
8. Professional knowledge, skills and values are shared appropriately in order to enrich the experience of children more widely.
9. Best practice requires reflection and a continuous search for improvement.

(Taken from the National Standards in Children's Care, Learning and Development.)

DfES Outcomes Framework

Following the publication of 'Every Child Matters – Changes for Children', the DfES with other partners created the Outcomes Framework. The Outcomes Framework is now part of the Ofsted Inspection Framework. Each of the five outcomes maps to one or more of the National Day Care Standards.

The outcomes are entitled:

- Helping children to **be healthy**
- Protecting children from harm or neglect and helping them to **stay safe**
- Helping children to **enjoy and achieve**
- Helping children to make a **postive contribution** to provision and wider community
- Helping children to achieve **economic well-being**.

The five outcomes are the targets for all children and young people. By using these outcomes in our work with children we will be improving their lifestyle and future chances.

Not all the outcomes will be evidenced in the CCLD qualifcation but reference can, and will, be made to some of the aims of the five outcomes. Parents, carers and families play an essential role in promoting the development of the whole child.

The Outcomes Framework records the expected outcome for every child and selects the aims for reaching the outcome; you, as the childcare practitioner, select the appropriate activities. As a childcare practitioner you must be aware of these outcomes and their specific aims and how you can produce evidence to show that you work towards them.

1. Be healthy
2. Stay safe
3. Enjoy and achieve
4. Make a positive contribution
5. Achieve economic well-being

DfES Common Core

Following the publication of 'Every Child Matters – Changes for Children', the DfES with other partners has produced a set of Common Core Skills and Knowledge for the children's workforce. This is to be used in all childcare settings to develop better and more effective services, producing a stronger and more knowledgeable workforce.

The knowledge and skills required for the Common Core are based in the following areas:

1. Communication
2. Child and young person development
3. Safeguarding the child
4. Supporting transition
5. Multi-agency working
6. Sharing information.

These areas of knowledge will be referred and mapped to your activities in this holistic assessment plan.

Evidence gathering methods

There are a variety of assessment methods that can be used for gathering evidence in an NVQ. The way evidence must be provided can be found at the end of each NVQ unit under the heading 'Unit Evidence Requirements'.

One assessment method – simulation – is rarely used in Children's Care, Learning and Development, and then only when it is clearly indicated in the evidence requirements, for example, element 202.2.

In NVQ units, most evidence must come from real work activities, observation being the most frequently used assessment method. Expert witnesses can supply additional evidence.

There are nine evidence gathering methods, as described below.

Direct Observation	Your assessor will observe you in the workplace on as many activities as possible. There should be a direct observation on each element.
Expert Witness Testimony	A named person from the workplace may write an Expert Witness Testimony. He or she must be occupationally competent and have a working knowledge of the Occupational Standards. This person must have worked for at least two years above the level for which he or she is going to testify competence. The expert witness must demonstrate continuous professional development.
Witness Testimony	A witness does not have to be qualified but can give a testimony on events that are difficult to observe. The witness's name must be entered onto the witness status list. The statement must indicate the relationship between the candidate and witness. Relatives and other close relationships cannot act as a witness.
Work Products	Work products that do not contravene the Data Protection Act can be used in the portfolio if you have contributed to their making. (Confidential records, photographs and children/family names must not appear in the portfolio.) They can be recorded as evidence and the location area must be recorded. The assessor and the work placement will agree the evidence.
Questioning	Questions may be oral or written but they must be recorded either by tape or on the question sheet.

Professional Discussion	Professional discussion takes the form of a structured review: you systematically analyse your work during a discussion. After your critical assessment you may look for ways of improvement.
Assignments, Projects and Others	These are set pieces of work where it is not always easy to secure the evidence through everyday activities.
Reflective Account	This can be a written or oral account whereby you reflect back on what you have done, how you did it and whether you could improve on it. If you give an oral reflective account it still has to be written down.
Accreditation of Prior Learning	For prior learning to be accredited there must be a proper process of assessing and mapping the previous evidence to the National Occupational Standards. Original certificates, e.g. First Aid, must be seen.

Confidentiality

You must take extreme care with confidentiality. Nowhere in the portfolio, whether paper evidenced or electronically collated, must it be possible to identify a child, young person, family, carer or work setting. When recording observations for evidence in your portfolio, you should not use the child's name but your own coding system. Confidential records from a workplace may not be placed in a portfolio. If it is necessary, assessors should read those documents in the workplace and write an observation about them, preserving the identity of the setting.

Contents of a portfolio

How you compile your portfolio and the contents contained within it will depend very much on the requirements of the Assessment Centre. Your assessor will help you with the required format.

Your portfolio, whether paper or electronic, should not contain any original certificates, paperwork from your setting or workshop handouts. All these items can be referred to and shown to your assessor, who will make reference as necessary.

All work submitted in your portfolio must be your own, signed and dated by you as proof of this.

Research and study skills

We each have a variety of different ways of learning. If we observe a baby learning, we can see him or her using all five senses. The first toy a baby can hold is:

Looked at	– seeing
Touched or held	– touching
Listened to	– hearing
Put in mouth to taste	– tasting
Smelt	– smelling

The baby may also squeal in delight, a form of communicating.

So this is how we learn. As we grow older, we refine our senses and develop a preferred way of learning.

You are about to enter an intense learning period in your life but at the same time you are going to be teaching others. You therefore need to think about your preferred learning style and, when working with children, you must remember to give them alternative ways of learning.

Let's think of the child first. Imagine you are trying to teach a little boy to understand what is meant by the number 2.

- You give him 2 bricks.
- You ask him to give you 2 bricks.
- You ask him to count to 2.
- You show him the number 2.
- You ask him to find 2 objects the same.
- You get him to add 1 + 1.

You have given him a variety of ways by which he could learn the meaning of the number 2: by seeing, by touching, by listening, by taking part and by doing his own research.

This is also how you learn, but you must decide how you learn best then use more than one way to reinforce your learning with repetition of new information.

Look at the following ideas.

Do you learn by?

Listening/hearing

To the tutor
To yourself talking aloud
To a tape
To a TV

Looking/seeing

By observing
By reading text
By looking at the Internet
By pictures, diagrams, plans, charts, colour
By looking at a TV programme

Looking and listening

Demonstrations
Videos, DVDs, TV
PowerPoint presentations
Handouts
Note making
Internet

Touching/tasting/smelling

Different textures
Rough/smooth, soft/hard, hot/cold, wet/dry
Tasting sweet/sour
Smelling good smells/bad smells

Communicating – being vocal

Two-way conversations
Questions and answers
Role play
Discussions and debates
By writing
By drawing

Once you have learnt which way you learn best, you must try to perfect it but, at the same time, practise other methods so that you become efficient in your use of time and skills.

- Look and listen but make notes.
- Look, listen and remember via creating picture images in your mind.
- Look, listen and find a special 'key point' by which to memorise.
- Look, listen and link the new knowledge to the old.
- Look, listen and be active by writing, drawing, researching, colouring, discussing or reading.
- Look, listen and attach memory hooks to specific facts.

How to write a bibliography

Why do you need to write a bibliography?

You need to give credit to the author of the book you have used for research if you have summarised or paraphrased any of his or her words, ideas, pictures or graphs, etc. This shows respect to the author and proves you are not stealing his or her work. It also allows the reader of your work to check your sources of evidence for accuracy.

You must include the following information in your biblography:

- name of author
- title of book, article, picture or chart
- place of publication
- name of publisher
- date of publication.

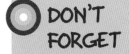

DON'T FORGET

If you do your bibliography on the computer, it will count towards your ICT Key Skill.

This is how it should look:

Last name	First name	Title of book underlined	Place of publication	Publisher	Date
Goodwin,	Ann.	The Good Nursery Guide.	Sutton:	Whitecals,	1999
comma	full stop	full stop	colon	comma	No punctuation

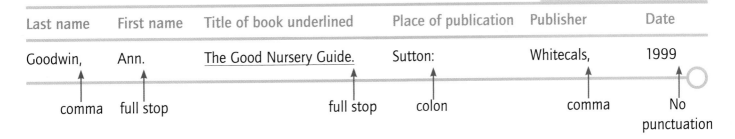

Your list should be in alphabetical order. You must do this for each piece of work. When quoting from or referring to a resource in your bibliography, you should include the page numbers in brackets in the text. Example 4 below shows a journal article and example 5 shows a web resource.

Bibliography example

1	Barry,	Ann.	Cooking For Children.	Croydon: NHS, 1999		
2	Dado,	Bill.	Communicate the Easy Way.	Byfleet: Davids, 2002		
3	Good,	John.	First Aid for You.	Reigate: Pogans, 2001		
4	Heath,	Roger.	Early Years Time.	Keeping Children happy,	May, 2004	pg 10
5	Under 5's Internet Download Childrens Skills				21.04.03	

Get organised

Once you have sorted out your learning style, you must think about self-organisation and the environment.

- Always have a pen and paper.
- Arrive on time.
- Work to your target dates.
- Hand your portfolio in on time.
- Plan time off for tests.
- Plan study time at home and work.
- Keep to a routine.
- Learn memory skills.
- Use a diary or year planner.
- Follow the timetable.
- Keep tutor notes and handouts in one folder.
- Keep your evidence and observations in a separate folder.
- Record the number of the page in pencil as you go.
- Record the page number on your tracking sheets.
- Evidence every performance criteria.
- Evidence every knowledge statement.

Before you know what has happened, you will have ... FINISHED!

Induction

A good induction introduces you to the apprenticeship framework.

Every effort should be made to attend induction to ensure you will understand the importance of:

- your training agreement **ERR**
- health and safety in the workplace, training centre and childcare settings **ERR**
- equal opportunities, anti-discrimination **ERR**
- contract of employment (or unemployment) **ERR**
- the apprenticeship framework **ERR**
- your job role and description
- your timetable and Individual Training Plan
- principles and values **ERR**
- confidentiality and data protection **ERR**
- legislation, policies and procedures
- gaining the apprentice framework holistically (using the workbook)
- building a portfolio
- personal safety.

Depending on the contents of your induction programme and the amount of information you research, you will be able to commence or even complete the indicated criteria towards the ERR unit. **ERR**

At the end of your probationary period (6 weeks) you should have been able to complete your ERR unit.

Tracking

All your individual pieces of work must be tracked, signed and dated by you.

Your assessment centre will give you a tracking system.

You **must** track:

- every performance criteria
- every knowledge evidence statement
- each Technical Certificate assignment and the related tasks
- each element and criteria of the Key Skills for both Application of Number and Communication
- the ERR unit.

1

Preparation for working with children

Chapter contents

Index to activities in Chapter 1

Children's development

You cannot work competently and successfully with children unless you know and understand all areas of child development.

Development means the way children grow and change. Development occurs in a set order or sequence; for example, babies sit before they walk, and walk before they run. As a childcare practitioner it is essential that you know the sequence and order of development, so that your expectations of children and the activities you set out are appropriate to their abilities and needs. By knowing the sequence of children's development you will know how to modify or extend activities according to the needs of individual children.

Whilst development generally occurs in a set order, children may develop at different rates. Children of the same age will not all necessarily reach the same development at the same age.

Finally, you must remember that children's development does not mean that you focus on different areas of development at different times; it encompasses all areas, all the time. Children do not develop in compartments; their development is **holistic**. In other words, whilst they are growing taller and stronger, they are also learning to communicate, to look at books and play with children; they are learning how to behave, what is hot and what is cold, what is big and what is small. They are growing across all development areas at the same time – holistically. These development areas are:

- physical
- intellectual
- social
- emotional
- linguistic.

In this first chapter on your journey to becoming a qualified child practitioner, you are going to carry out some research into the holistic growth and development of children and young people.

Before starting this work, however, you must familiarise yourself with the principles and values of the childcare sector and ensure that all your work with children reflects best practice and supports the rights of the child.

Principles and Values

Let's start by looking at the three principles and nine values that underpin the practitioner's work with children in the care learning and development sector in which you work.

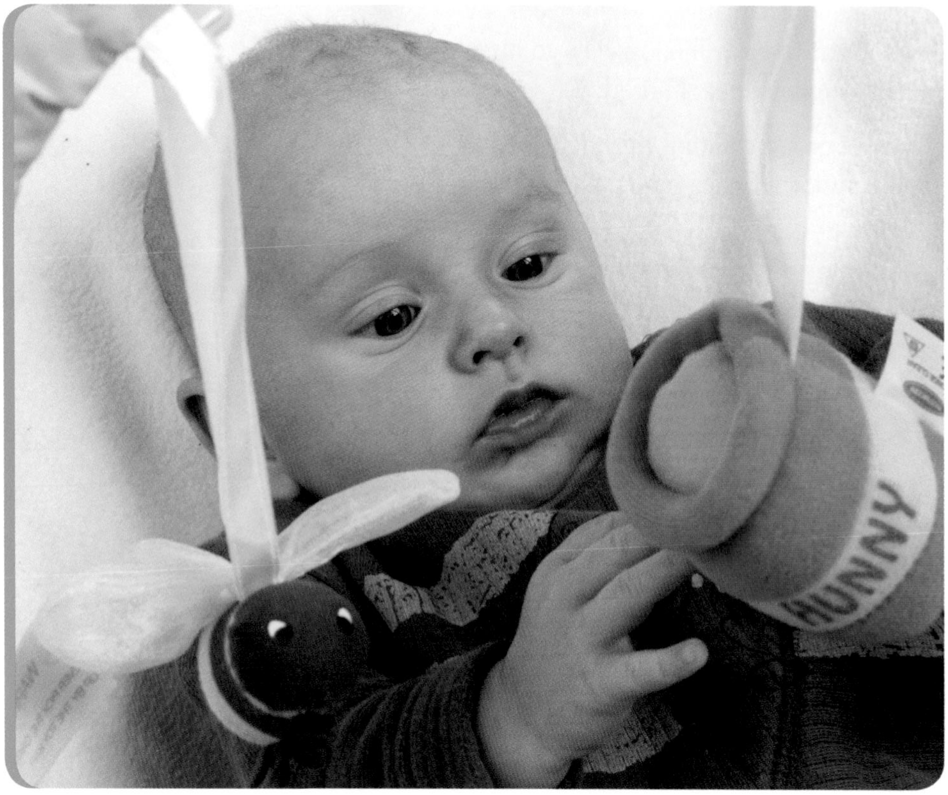

Activity 1.1 Technical Certificate Unit 001 Task A

T.Cert 001 Task A

The National Occupational Standards (NOS) are underpinned by three principles and nine values.

- List each principle and value, using templates T01.1–T01.2.
- Give one example of how each principle and value might be applied in a childcare environment.

You may complete the second part of this assignment whilst you are working through your apprenticeship programme, as you carry out different activities with the children in your setting.

Principles and Values 1, 2, 3

Common Core 1, 2, 3, 6

Outcomes Framework 1, 2, 3, 4, 5

EGM Assignment

TARGET DATE:

Assignment 001 Principles and values underpinning the Children's Care, Learning and Development sector

T01.1

Task A

The National Occupational Standards are underpinned by three principles and nine values. List each principle and value in the grid below. Give one example of how each might be applied in a childcare environment.

	Principle	Example of how it is applied
1		
2		
3		
	Value	**Example of how it is applied**
1		
2		
3		

T01.2

	Value	Example of how it is applied
4		
5		
6		
7		
8		
9		

You are going to be working as part of a team. This may be in a new setting or you may have been in the childcare setting for some time. Either way, it is important to know the behaviour that will be expected of you, your roles and responsibilities, your rights and the rights of your colleagues.

You can expect to be respected and to be accepted as part of the team.

NVQ 207 1

NVQ 207 2

Activity 1.2 Team work

Carry out some research into the workings of a team, its attitudes and behaviours, codes of practice and conduct. Check the records that have been kept in a childcare setting and the requirements of the Data Protection Act 1998. Set your personal target for completing this work.

TARGET DATE:

Activity 1.3 Team work

NVQ 207 1 3
NVQ 207 K207H01 K207H05

EGM ERR

When working in a team you must ensure that you work within the policies and procedures of your setting, the principles and values of the sector, and the legal responsibilities and requirements, at both the personal and team level.

Write down the legal and organisational requirements of:

- equality
- diversity
- discrimination
- rights

when working in teams.

TARGET DATE:

You will shortly start work on NVQ Unit 203, but just before you start this work, let's make sure you really understand your responsibilities and those of your colleagues within the setting.

Activity 1.4 Team work

Speak to your manager or line manager and clarify his or her expectations of you as a team member.

With his or her help, state the purpose of the team, its aims and objectives.

NVQ 207 1 1
NVQ 207 K207H02

- Draw an organisational chart showing the lines of reporting within your setting.
- Write out your role and responsibilities in the team:

NVQ 207 1 2

  a) your role and responsibilities to others
  b) how your role and responsibilities contribute to the overall objectives and purpose of the team.

- State how you will be able to access the policies and procedures of your setting should you need to refer to them.

NVQ 207 K207H04

TARGET DATE:

You are now going to start working on NVQ Unit 203. This unit is key to your apprenticeship framework and work with children. In this unit you need to know about the development of children aged 0–16 years.

NVQ 203

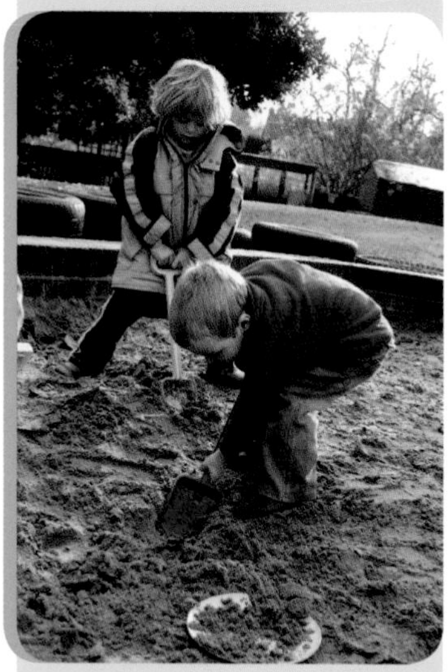

When you work with children it is essential that you know and understand their development and are able to observe and assess their achievements, abilities and needs.

Before you carry out any activities, it is worth bearing in mind a few key thoughts.

As a childcare practitioner, you will be supporting the children in their growth and development, therefore, you must know how to stimulate them, interact with them during activities, modify or extend their play, and keep them safe, happy and interested. It is through your encouragement that they will learn.

This means there is a lot of responsibility allocated to you. The only way to prove your competency is to ensure that you understand all areas of child development – so do ask for help and support from staff as and when you need it. Then you can use your new-found knowledge for the benefit of yourself and the children you work with.

For your own development you will be working with:

NVQ 204

NVQ 203 1
2
3
4

Once you have learnt about children's growth and development areas, and begin to have an understanding of how each area relies upon the others and their interconnectedness, you will start to have a broad understanding of **holistic development**. To confirm this new learning you need to observe children at play. This will help to reinforce your learning and also teach you new facts about children and young people.

DON'T FORGET

Before you start work you must read through NVQ Units 203 and 204, so that you understand what is expected of you.

As you watch, listen, supervise and observe children, the knowledge gained from the observations will help you when you plan their future learning.

You must try to incorporate several performance criteria, elements and knowledge understanding from different units into one piece of work.

This is called **holistic assessment** or **action planning**.

Hints & Tips

Enough of tips and hints – it's nearly time to act! But first be wise: read and follow the suggestions below.

- Use your own learning style (refer back to the Induction section on page 16 if you have forgotten about this).
- Wheneverpossible make use of support systems to develop your practice.
- Whenyou gain new knowledge and skills, use them to improve your practice.
- Alwayswork within the context of the principles and values of the childcare sector.
- Contributeto forming positive relationships with children and adults. You can do this by listening to them, giving your full attention, showing positive body language, responding appropriately to their conversation, and asking questions to confirm understanding or extend their knowledge and thoughts.

NVQ 204 K2P54

NVQ 204 1
2

Principles and Values

NVQ 201 1
2

Whether you are employed in a childcare setting or not, it is important that you understand your role and responsibilities as a team member. You also need to play your part effectively so that other team members can rely on you.

NVQ 207 1
2

NVQ Unit 207 is an optional unit, but as you work through your apprenticeship you will need to both support and rely on colleagues, just as they will need to support and rely on you. It is therefore worth considering 'Shall I complete Unit 207 as an extra unit?' After all, you have started it already!

We all have to be good team players – they are always needed!

DON'T FORGET

Work in partnership with your assessor and the key worker of the childcare setting.

Create the basis of your bibliography then, when you carry out some research, add the name of the source and other details to your list.

Finally, remember the target dates on your Individual Training Plan (ITP). Discuss with your assessor the date when each of the activities in this workbook need to be completed. Plan the target date of the activities to enable you to keep within the target dates of your ITP.

ALWAYS complete all work by the target date!

We are going to start with an activity that will help you to understand how children's stages of growth and development are holistic and interconnected.

This one activity will cover tasks and assignments from both the NVQ, the Technical Certificate, knowledge and understanding from various units and Chapter 2 ('Child and young person development') of the Common Core.

Activity 1.5 Technical Certificate Unit 003 Task Ai

T.Cert 003 Task A i

The term 'development' refers to the way in which children and young people grow and change.

NVQ 201 K2D39

Common Core 2

Using templates T02.1–T02.4, make use of a variety of research and learning methods (including observation) to record the holistic development of children and young people across four age ranges:

- 0–3 years
- 3–7 years
- 7–12 years
- 12–16 years.

As you fill in the templates, show that you know the main areas of growth and development and the broad pattern of development in each age range. Identify the development and give one example for each age group.

NVQ 203 K2D47

Hints & Tips

Include in your answer all the Knowledge Understanding numbers recorded on the right-hand side of this page.

NVQ 203 K2D47
K2D45
K2D46
NVQ 206 K2D87
NVQ 208 K2D115

TARGET DATE:

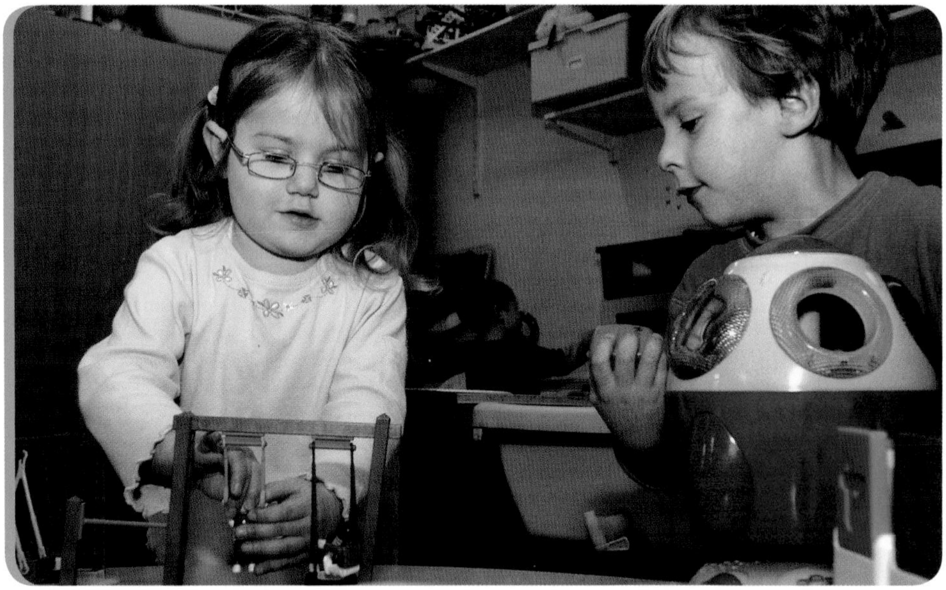

Assignment 003 Child and young person development

T02.1

Task Ai

Age: 0–3 years	Physical development	Communication and intellectual development	Social, emotional and behavioural development

T02.2

Age: 3–7 years	Physical development	Communication and intellectual development	Social, emotional and behavioural development

T02.3

Age: 7–12 years	Physical development	Communication and intellectual development	Social, emotional and behavioural development

T02.4

Age: 12–16 years	Physical development	Communication and intellectual development	Social, emotional and behavioural development

Activity 1.6 Key Skills Communication Level 1

K.Skill Com L1

NVQ 203 K2D48 K2D49 K2D50

Whilst you have been researching the development of children aged 0–16 years, you have been completing some of the performance criteria for the Communication Key Skill Level 1. Let's look at how you have achieved this.

Read relevant material

K.Skill Com C1.2 1

In your bibliography, record all the books, papers, videos and Internet sites that you used to help you research child development (0–16 years).

In your Key Skill log book, state why the books and other materials were relevant.

Identify accurately the main points and ideas

K.Skill Com C1.2 2

In Activity 1.5 you selected the main points and ideas about the holistic development of children aged 0–16 years. Now cross-reference this information (evidence) to your Key Skill log book.

Use the information to suit your purpose

K.Skill Com C1.2 3

Once you have written out the developmental progress of children aged 0–16 years, you have used the information for a purpose. Remember to state the purpose in your log book.

Hints & Tips

Ask your assessor to help you cross-reference your work to your Key Skill log book, write the index and complete the numbering of the pages in your portfolio.

Present information in a format that suits your purpose

K.Skill Com C1.3 1

Present your information as requested in Activity 1.5. State why it is appropriate and cross-reference to your Key Skill log book.

Spell, punctuate and use grammar accurately

K.Skill Com C1.3 2

Check your work for accurate spellings, punctuation and grammar. If you have misspelt a word, leave it in place and (in a different coloured ink) write the correct spelling above.

If you have written your work in rough first, add this as an evidence draft. Cross-reference to your Key Skill log book.

Use at least one image

K.Skill Com Image

NVQ 208 K2D115

Design a chart showing the basic outline of the expected pattern of development for children aged 0–3 years, including the acceptable range and recognised limits. You may use words to explain each illustration.

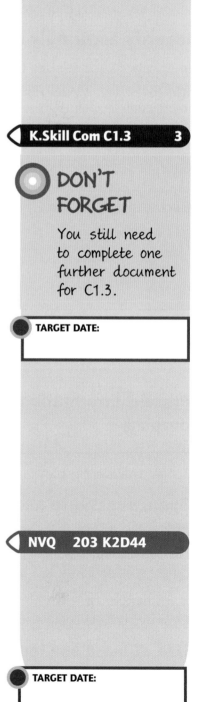

K.Skill Com C1.3 3

Make your meaning clear

Check the work you have done is grammatically correct, including the punctuation. Show evidence of any mistakes you have corrected.

Cross-reference your work to your Key Skill log book.

Well done! You have completed two elements of Communication Level 1 whilst completing knowledge evidence for both the NVQ and Technical Certificate.

DON'T FORGET

You still need to complete one further document for C1.3.

TARGET DATE:

Activity 1.7 Influences on child development

NVQ 203 K2D44

Children's development can be influenced by different circumstances. These may be happenings before or after birth.

When children are born with a condition that affects their growth or development – hearing loss, for example – it is called a genetic or hereditary factor.

When a child's development is influenced by external factors, such as bullying, it is said to be due to environmental conditions.

Use templates T03.1–T03.2 to record:

- the major factors that may influence growth and development
- some conditions that may affect growth and development.

A child's rate of growth and development is influenced by many external factors.

TARGET DATE:

Genetic/hereditary influences on children's growth and development **T03.1**

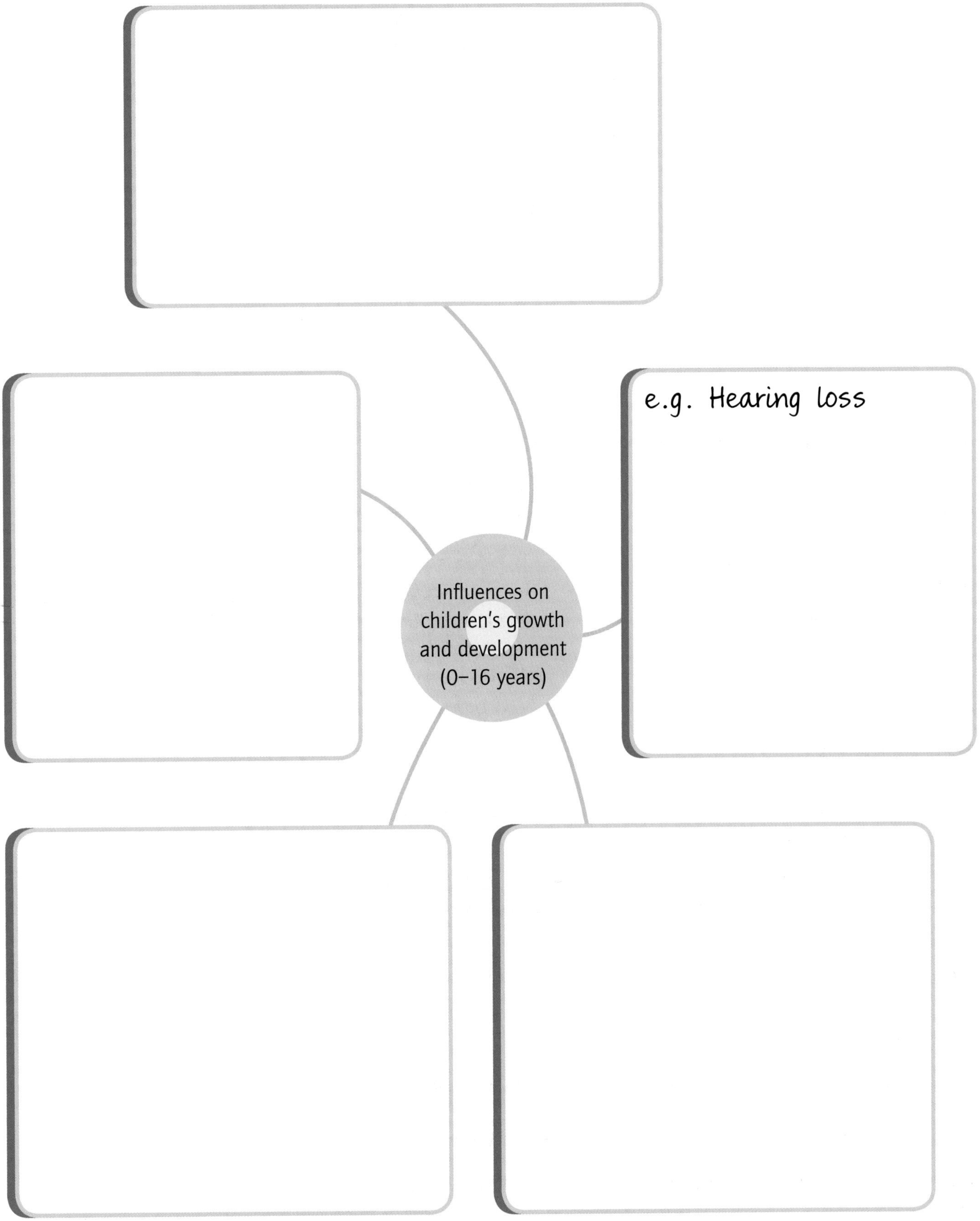

Environmental conditions that may affect children's growth and development **T03.2**

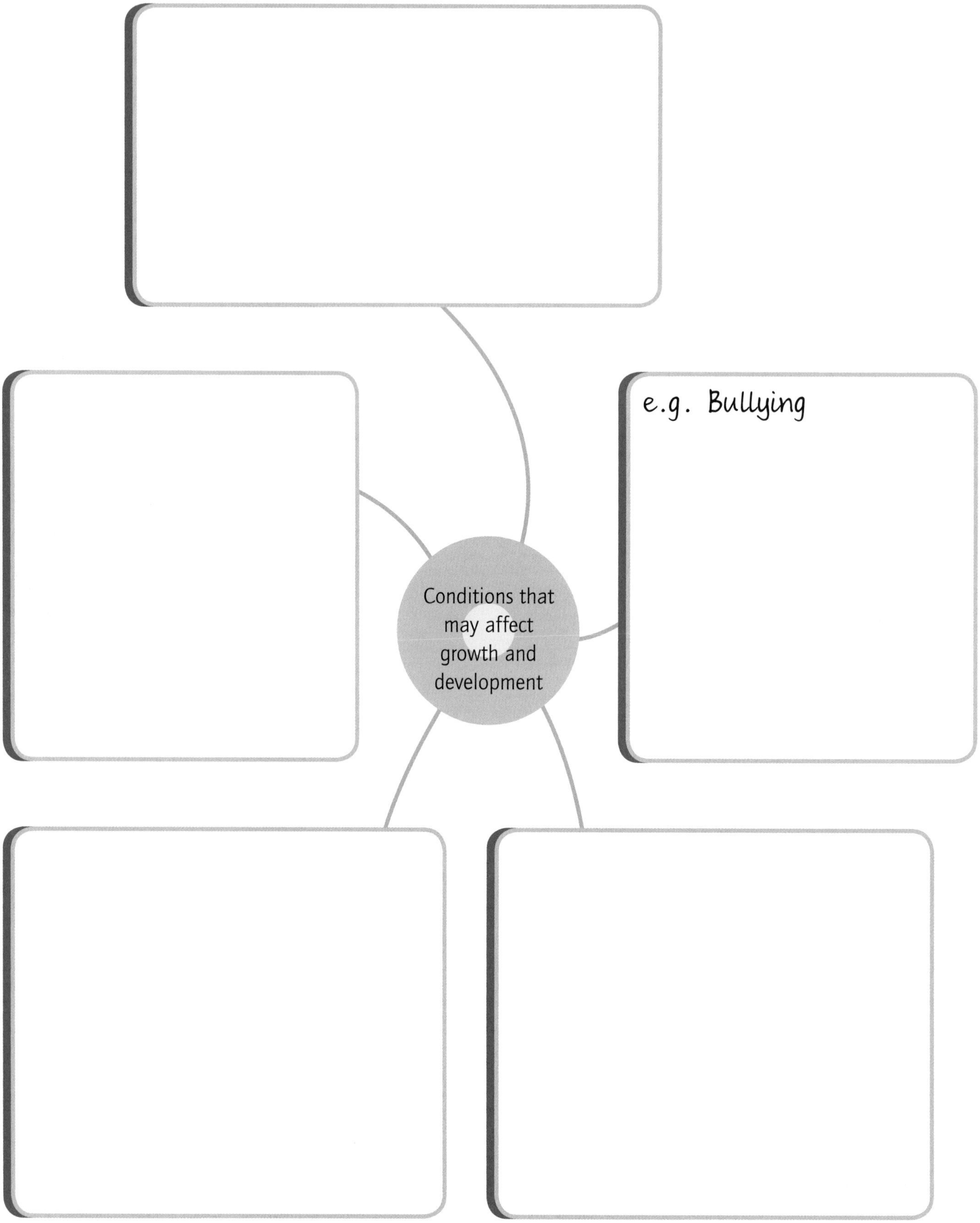

Hereditary factors will impact on a child's biological maturity, with the family culture and systems influencing each child differently.

Environmental factors will influence a child's development to a greater or lesser degree, depending on the external stimuli, encouragement, care and protection that the child is given.

For a child to develop, he or she must learn to explore, investigate, question and solve problems. The child can do all of this through the (well thought out) medium of play.

You will shortly be setting out activities for children, to promote and support their developmental progress. It is therefore essential that you first learn about the stages and value of play.

Activity 1.8 Play

Carry out some personal research about play. Use books and the Internet, and attend workshops. Complete your bibliography.

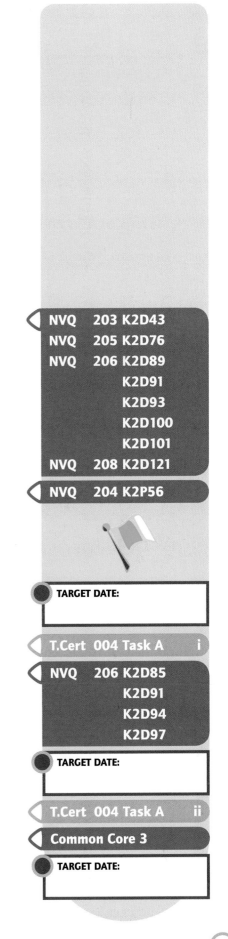

NVQ 203 K2D43
NVQ 205 K2D76
NVQ 206 K2D89
K2D91
K2D93
K2D100
K2D101
NVQ 208 K2D121

Give yourself a date by which you must complete your research into play.

NVQ 204 K2P56

Inform your assessor.

Having carried out some personal research on play, now complete an assignment on play to prove your new knowledge.

TARGET DATE:

Activity 1.9 Technical Certificate Unit 004 Task Ai

T.Cert 004 Task A i

NVQ 206 K2D85
K2D91
K2D94
K2D97

Give three reasons why play is important in helping children and young people learn.

TARGET DATE:

Activity 1.10 Technical Certificate Unit 004 Task Aii

T.Cert 004 Task A ii

Common Core 3

Fill in templates T04.1–T04.3 to show that you can identify different types of play for different age groups, how play can stimulate development and learning, and what activities, equipment and opportunities encourage different development, behaviour and learning.

TARGET DATE:

Assignment 004 Supporting children's play and learning

T04.1

Task Aii

TYPE OF PLAY	ACTIVITY	RESOURCES	DEVELOPMENT/BEHAVIOUR/ LEARNING
Physical (fine or gross motor skills)			
0–3 years	1	1	1
3–7 years	2	2	2
Creative			
3–7 years	1	1	1
7–12 years	2	2	2

T04.2

TYPE OF PLAY	ACTIVITY	RESOURCES	DEVELOPMENT/BEHAVIOUR/ LEARNING
Drama/Imaginative/Symbolic			
12–16 years	1	1	1
Provide a second example for 12–16 years	2	2	2
Construction			
3–7 years	1	1	1
7–12 years	2	2	2

T04.3

TYPE OF PLAY	ACTIVITY	RESOURCES	DEVELOPMENT/BEHAVIOUR/ LEARNING
Heuristic/Exploitative/Investigation			
0–3 years	1	1	1
3–7 years	2	2	2
Outdoor			
Any age	1	1	1
Provide a second example for any age group	2	2	2

You have recently spent some time learning about children's play. You should now realise that play is to children what work is to adults.

When children are not sleeping or eating they are generally playing. They learn through play by investigating, exploring and experimenting. It is the responsibility of the carer to ensure that the child remains safe whilst playing.

As a carer you need to learn about safety and how to carry out risk assessments. You probably carry out risk assessments already without realising it. For example:

The gate to your garden has been vandalised overnight and the safety catch is now broken. You wanted to take the children into the garden to play. You thought: 'Shall I take the children into the garden and hope they don't open the gate?' You assessed the risk and decided it was high risk (too risky!). It was likely that the children would open the gate, escape and possibly come to harm. Your decision was no garden play until the gate was repaired. Well done!

This risk assessment was probably carried out in your head, but whenever possible they **must** be written down.

Activity 1.11 Technical Certificate Unit 002 Task Aiii

T.Cert 002 Task A iii

NVQ 202 K2P18
NVQ 205 1 4

EGM Work Product

Common Core 3

Carry out some training and research into risk assessments.

Now complete the following Technical Certificate assignment:

- Write a brief account of what a risk assessment is. Conduct a risk assessment for an activity/area in which you are involved, using your organisation's documentation and procedures.

Activity 1.12 Technical Certificate Unit 002 Task Aiv

T.Cert	002 Task A	iv
NVQ	202 1	3
EGM	Work Product	

TARGET DATE:

Outline what you can do to reduce the hazards by adapting your chosen activity/area to meet the needs and abilities of children and young people in the environment in which you are working.

Conclusion

In this chapter you have learnt about the principles and values in childcare which will help you to work respectfully with children.

You have learnt the stages and value of play.

You have gained an insight into children's growth and development.

And, by no means of least importance, you have experienced risk assessments.

You will use this new knowledge and these experiences again as you continue through this workbook.

Preparation for a professional observation

2

Chapter contents

Index to activities in Chapter 2

As a new apprentice you have already learnt about some important topics – let's reminisce for a minute.

Play

Play, you have learnt, is the child's most powerful teaching tool. Play satisfies a child's curiosity. Children explore, investigate and learn using all five senses. Well-planned play promotes the development of physical, intellectual, emotional and social skills. Play cannot be wrong, therefore children cannot fail, and this, of course, helps to improve their self-esteem.

With play there is repetition, with repetition there is learning.

Play is for all ages, therefore the competent child carer plans play for all abilities and needs.

Risk assessment

NVQ 208 K2H124

Risk assessment should be carried out daily, checking that the activity you plan for the children is safe and the environment is as free from hazards as possible.

Risk assessments should be written on the setting's Risk Assessment template and filled in for future use (for example, at inspection or if an accident occurs).

For speed, convenience and safety, risk assessments may be carried out in different ways:

- silently, in your head (checking out the environment)
- by writing the risks and recording the hazards (this could be discussed and some hazards eliminated)
- by planning ahead and suggesting the risks, e.g. on an outing.

The aim of the risk assessment is to minimise the hazard, thus reducing the health and safety risks that children are subject to in the environment.

Development

NVQ 203 K2D46

You have also completed the basic growth and developmental milestones of children and young people. You understand that the pattern of development generally remains the same but the rate of development varies with the individual child.

Hints & Tips

It is essential that, as a childcare practitioner, you are familiar with the usual pattern of development and the effects of influences, so that you can identify children who may not be following the usual pattern (thereby requiring additional or extended support).

Common Core 3

This knowledge of growth and development will help you with one of the most important skills that a childcare practitioner has to use: observation.

Using observation skills

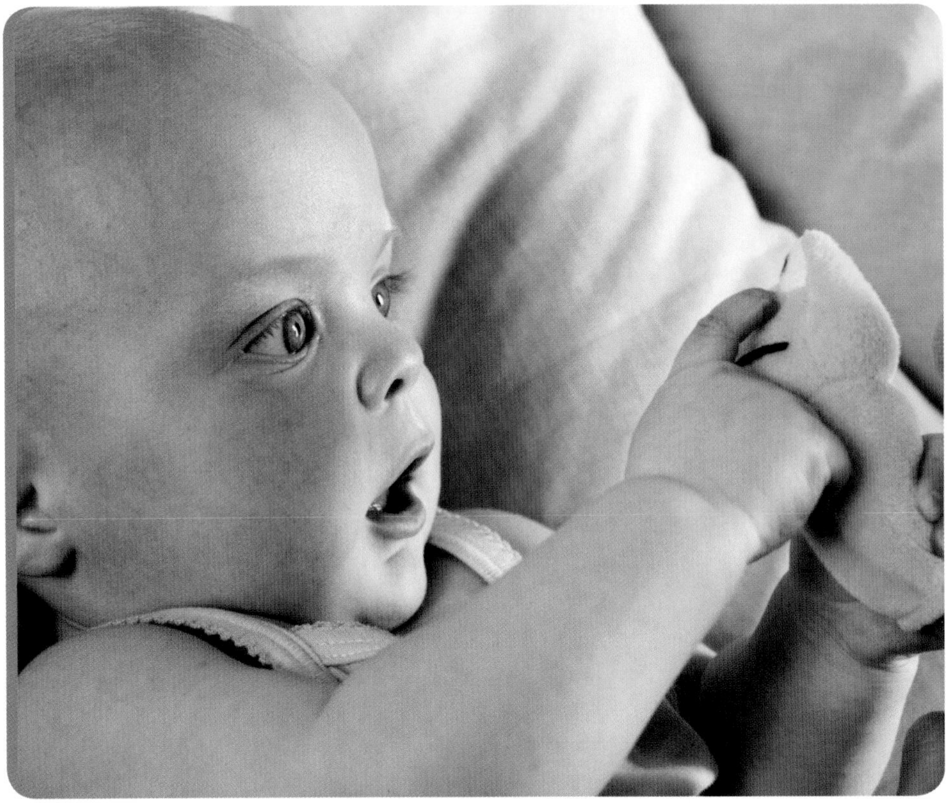

Look at the picture opposite.

What do you observe?

Amazement on face.

One hand clasped round frog.

Index finger pointing at eyes.

What else can you add?

What else do you see?

What extra details can you record?

Common Core 2

To be a competent childcare practitioner you must be a skilful observer. This means being able to observe the safety of the environment and the children at all times. It also means being able to carry out detailed observations of children to find out their developmental stage.

Observation is not just watching. It is the combined use of all your senses and skills.

Looking

You see that the child is playing with a bus.

Writing or recording

The child is pushing the bus back and forth, changing the use of his hands as he pushes it around.

Listening

He makes the sound of the bus's engine. He changes the sound when he crashes the bus!

Thinking

'It would be nice if he had a roadway on which to push the bus.'

Good quality observations are a key function of top quality childcare provision.

Skilful observation will give you an understanding of each child's individual needs, enable you to see and share each child's personal achievements, and allow you to assess what is the next stage in his or her development.

You need to know which technique or format to use when recording the observation. There are four main categories/techniques from which to choose – each category then has many formats. You need to learn all of these to ensure you choose the correct format for the focus of the observation.

Principles and Values

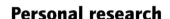

Personal research

It is time to carry out thorough personal research into child observations – look at books, attend workshops and training sessions, download from the Internet, speak to colleagues and follow the policies of your setting.

Give yourself a discipline boundary and a date by which you will have completed this research.

TARGET DATE:

Your first aim is to learn about the children in your group, their interests and capabilities. Once you know their capabilities you will be able to plan the next stage of their learning.

NVQ 203 4

Before you can plan and provide accurate information on the developmental stage of each child, you must observe, assess and judge his or her:

- gross and fine motor skills

NVQ 203 1
NVQ 206 3
4

- social, emotional and behavioural development

NVQ 203 2
NVQ 206 2
5

- intellectual and communication skills.

NVQ 203 4
NVQ 206 1

Activity 2.1 Key Skills Communication Level 1

K.Skill Com L1

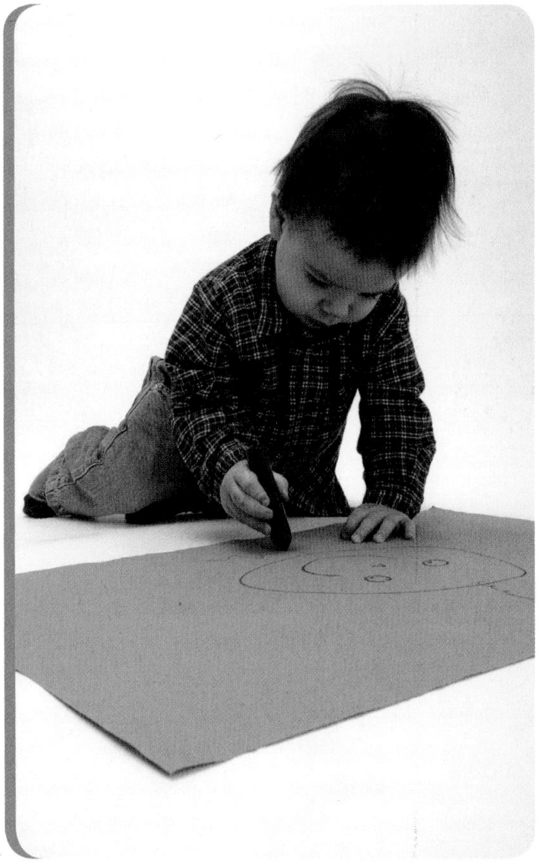

You are now going to start the preparation for child observations. At the same time you will be able to complete the Communication Key Skill and start the Application of Number Key Skill.

When you carry out observations you must continue to use everyday care routines to support the children's development, providing hands-on activities that allow children to explore, manipulate materials and encourage their creativity.

NVQ 203 K2D48 7
8
11

EGM Expert Witness Testimony

Try to plan some time with your line manager or key worker to have a one-to-one discussion about the forthcoming observations.

K.Skill Com C1.1 1
2

Approach the line manager with courtesy and respect, using his or her preferred name.

NVQ 201 4 1

- Keep the notes you make.
- Keep records of your discussion and decisions.

K.Skill Com C1.3 1, 2, 3

This could be your second document for Key Skill Communication C1.3.

Make clear that you wish to discuss the carrying out of child observations on children within your group, across different development areas. This will help you to contribute towards appropriate activities and experiences to meet their developmental needs.

NVQ 203 1 2 3 4

Emphasise your intention:

- to gain permission for all child observations according to the policy of the setting
- to allow children to practise activities before being observed
- to observe children across different development areas/activities
- to use similar activities again, but decreasing or increasing the complexity to modify the children's learning.

EGM Expert Witness Testimony

Whilst speaking with your line manager:

- use the key features of effective communication
- remember the difference between communicating with adults and children

NVQ 201 K2C6

NVQ 201 K2C7

- demonstrate that you value your line manager's views

  NVQ 201 K2C8

- reassure your line manager that you will keep information confidential and adhere to the settings' policy

  NVQ 201 K2M11 K2M12

- give the line manager your full attention when you are communicating with him or her

  NVQ 201 2 1

- respond confidently, being knowledgable about child observation activities, but show that you have listened to your line manager's views by giving further information when requested; clarify any misunderstandings that might occur

  NVQ 201 2 3 5 4

- exchange information with your line manager using appropriate communication methods, resolving any difficulties that may be experienced

  NVQ 201 4 3 4 5

- record your conversation with the line manager in a reflective account, demonstrating that you have understood.

  NVQ 201 2 2

  EGM Reflective Account

Hints & Tips

Using the Key Skill standards as a guide, ask your line manager to complete an Expert Witness Testimony recording the specifics of your discussion. Gain a date and signature.

EGM Expert Witness Testimony

TARGET DATE:

Activity 2.2 Questions 1–9

Q1) How did you show in your discussion with the line manager that you valued his or her individual needs and preferences? **NVQ 201 4 2; NVQ 201 K2C8**

Q2) Why is it important to convince your line manager and team that you will keep any shared information confidential? **NVQ 201 K2M11**

Q3) When may you have to break a confidence? **NVQ 201 K2M11**

Q4) Describe the key features of effective communication. Why is it important to model this with both adults and children? **NVQ 201 K2C6**

Q5) There are times when communication may be difficult – for example, if English is not the spoken language or there are reading/writing difficulties. How would you overcome these difficulties? **NVQ 201 K2C9**

Q6) If you had a disagreement with an adult, how would you resolve this? **NVQ 201 K2C10**

Q7) Why is it important to communicate positively with children and their families? **NVQ 201 K2C13**

Q8) Explain how a child's ability to communicate can affect his or her behaviour. **NVQ 201 K2C14**

Q9) Why is it important to give all children the opportunity to speak? How can you do this in a group?

NVQ 201 K2C3

EGM Questioning

TARGET DATE:

You have now completed the Communication Level 1 Key Skill. This would be a good time to complete Application of Number Level 1, then you will have gained three certificates towards your Apprenticeship: ERR, Communication and Application of Number Key Skills.

Well done – you could say you are nearly halfway there!

Activity 2.3 Key Skills Application of Number Level 1

K.Skill AON L1

Imagine that you are based in a 63-place childcare centre accommodating children aged 3 months to 5 years.

You are registered for:

- 15 children under 2 years
- 16 children under 3 years
- 32 children under 5 years.

Your placement, Anytown Childcare Centre, is a pretty red-brick building with five play rooms, a kitchen, bathroom, other utilities, garden and playground.

Full day care centres have to plan their days according to:

- National Day Care Standards
- Birth to Three Matters
- Early Years Foundation Stage
- the routine of the day
- the chosen activities of the children (to some extent).

The number of children on the register is exactly 100. There is a waiting list of 24 children. You have been asked to work in Alligator room.

Pretend the building just described is the one you are working in. Work through the following tasks to gain evidence towards your Key Skill units.

K.Skill N1 1 1

Anytown Childcare Centre – Plan A

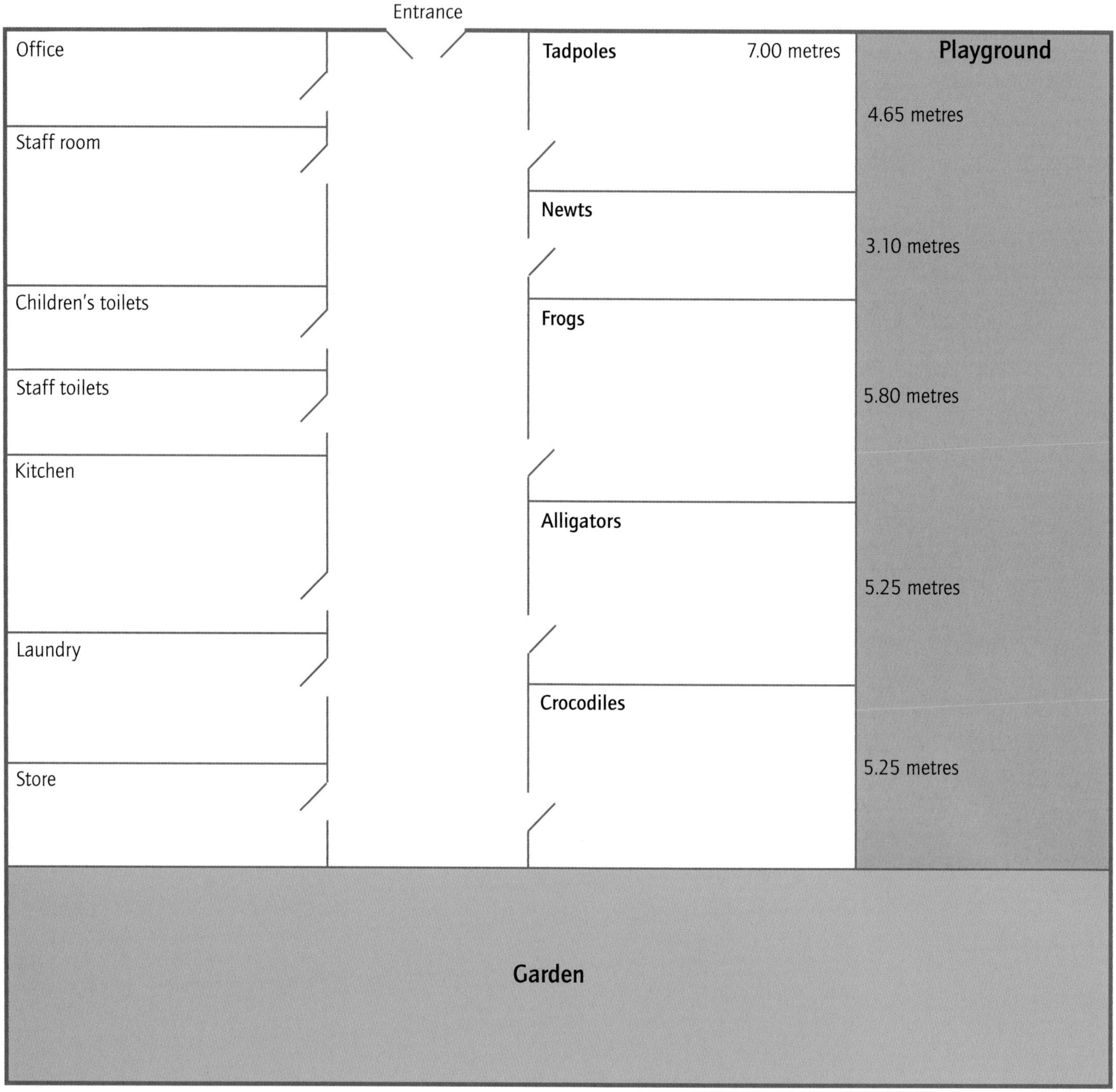

Plan A

KS1. Using the National Day Care Standards as your guide, work out how many staff you will need for each of the age groups the centre is registered for. What is the total number of staff?

Show your working out and ask your assessor to help you cross-reference this to your Key Skill log book.

K.Skill N1 1 1

NVQ 202 K2P25

K.Skill N1 1 2

KS2. Look at Plan A of Anytown Childcare Centre. One wall of each play room is 7 metres. The second dimension for each room is written on the plan. Work out the size of each room and record your answers in square metres. Show your working out and state why your results make sense.

K.Skill N1 1 1a
2 2

KS3. You know that the total number of registered children in the centre can only be 63. Using the National Day Care Standards, work out how many children can be accommodated in each room, keeping them in age groups. You will need to work to the nearest whole number.

K.Skill N1 2 2
1 1a

KS4. Having established how many children are in each room, use a calculator to work out the percentage of children in the centre. (Remember, the total number of children in the centre is 63.)

K.Skill N1 1 1b

KS5. Record the age of the children in each room.

K.Skill N1 2 1a

KS6. How many staff are required in each room?

K.Skill N1 2 1a

KS7. The manager of Anytown Childcare Centre wanted to order some new toys so last week she arranged for a survey to find out the popularity of different childcare activities. The results can be seen in Figures 1a and 1b (below and on page 58).

a) Which is the most popular indoor activity?

K.Skill N1 2 1a

b) Which is the most popular outdoor activity?

Show your working out and record it in your Key Skill log book.

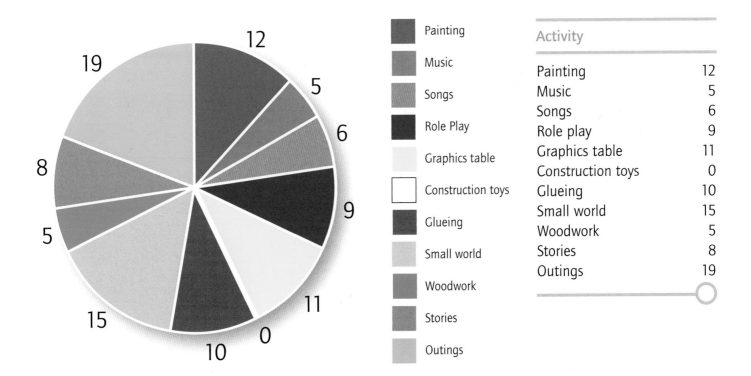

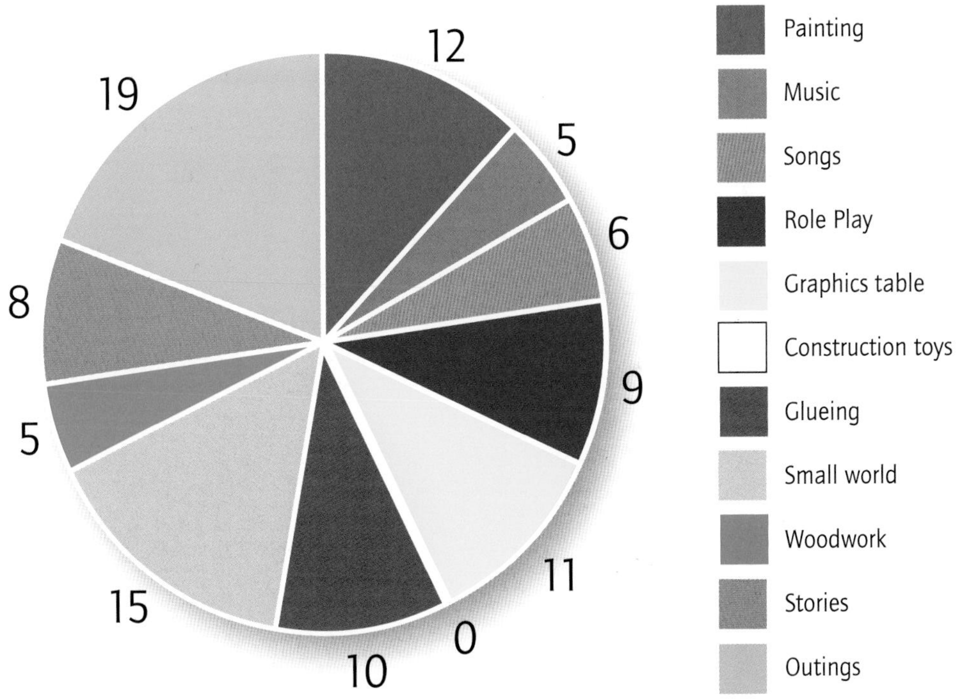

Activity	
Painting	12
Music	5
Songs	6
Role play	9
Graphics table	11
Construction toys	0
Glueing	10
Small world	15
Woodwork	5
Stories	8
Outings	19

Figure 1a: Indoor play activities, Anytown Childcare Centre

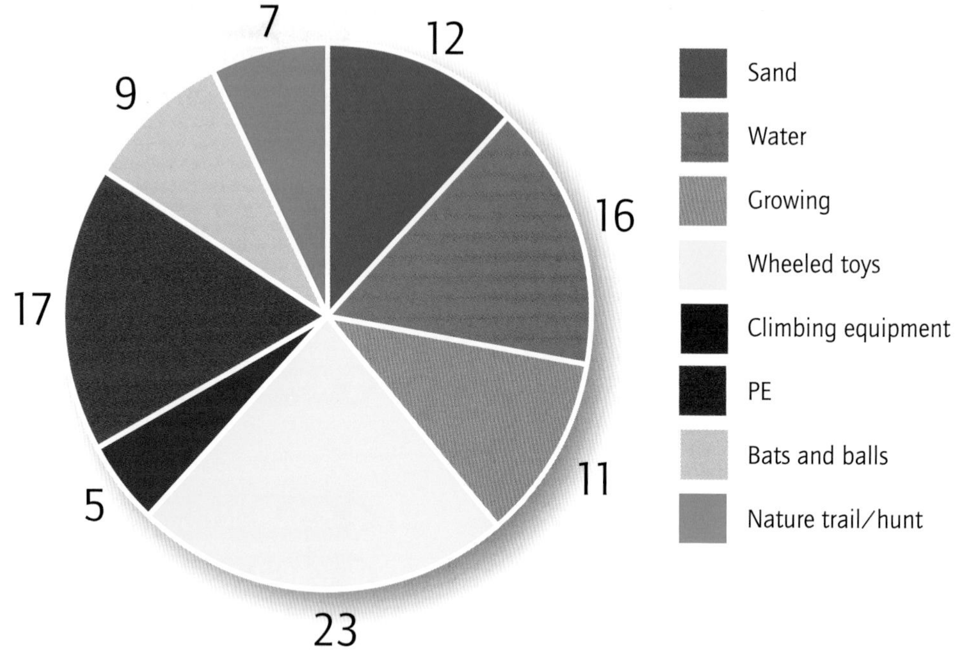

Activity	
Sand	12
Water	16
Growing	11
Wheeled toys	23
Climbing equipment	5
PE	17
Bats and balls	9
Nature trail/hunt	7

Figure 1b: Outdoor play activities

KS8. If there were 48 children in the setting, what percentage would play with water?

K.Skill N1 2 1b

KS9. If there were 60 children in the setting, what fraction would play with small world toys?

K.Skill N1 2 1b

KS10. To buy new climbing equipment you need to have 30 per cent of the children choosing it as their favourite activity. How many more children must choose climbing equipment?

K.Skill N1 2 1b

KS11. Carry out your own survey with a group of children, asking them which is their favourite activity. (Play activities are to be from your own setting. State the number of children you surveyed – this must be 10 or more.)

Present your findings in:

K.Skill N1 3 3

- a table
- a graph
- a pie chart.

Describe what your results mean.

K.Skill N1 3 4

KS12. To enable the children to grow strong muscles and bones and have good health, physical exercise is recommended as a daily activity. According to the survey, 17 per cent of the children asked enjoy PE.

It is important that more children enjoy physical exercise. You are required to plan an activity with different physical exercises that will last approximately 20–30 minutes. List the activities and mark on a timetable how long each activity will last. Look at the daily routine for Anytown Childcare Centre on the next page and state what time you plan to carry out the PE session.

NVQ 203 1 3
4
NVQ 203 K2D48 17
K.Skill N1 1 1

KS13. Carry out the PE session and observe the children using a checklist you have designed.

NVQ 204 1 2
EGM Direct Observation
K.Skill N1 3 1

KS14. Evaluate your results by adding together the number of children who could carry out each exercise. From the total number of children observed, show in fractions and decimals the proportion of children who could do each exercise. Remember to identify any new knowledge and skills that will be useful in your work.

NVQ 204 2 2

KS15. Look at Anytown Childcare Centre's daily routine again. You have been asked to complete a daily routine for your group in Alligator room. You will see that some of the basic personal needs have been entered for you.

K.Skill N1 2 2

Complete the daily routine, being sure to include activities that give the children quiet periods and explaining why you have put in the quiet periods at that time.

NVQ 205 K2D77
NVQ 205 4 2

KS17. At midday the temperature reading is taken in each room for health and safety reasons. Figure 2 below shows the readings in degrees Celsius for three of the rooms (Newts, Tadpoles and Frogs) for the last 11 days.

Day	Newts	Tadpoles	Frogs
1	23.5	21	22
2	24	21.5	22
3	23	22	22.6
4	23.5	21.3	23.5
5	23	21	23.6
6	23	21.2	24.2
7	23.5	22.5	23.6
8	23.6	23.3	22.6
9	23.5	23.3	22.8
10	23.5	23	24
11	22.5	24	23.6

Figure 2: Room temperature readings in degrees Celsius

Work out the average temperature for each room over the 11 days. (Average = mean.)

K.Skill N1 2 1c

Anytown Childcare Centre – Daily Routine

7.45	Open centre H&S check	
8.00am–9.00am	Children arrive, have quiet play Breakfast, milk feeds Toilet, nappy changes	
9.15am–10.15am		Observations by staff or apprentices
10.15am–10.30am	Hand washing Drinks, snacks or self-service time for children	
10.30am–12.00pm		Observations by staff or apprentices
12.00pm–1.30pm	Hand washing Toilet, nappy changes Lunch, drinks; sleep, rest time or quiet activities	
1.30pm–3.00pm		
3.00pm–3.15pm	Hand washing Drinks, snacks Toilet, nappy changes	
3.15pm–4.15pm		
4.15pm–4.45pm	Hand washing Tea Toilet, nappy changes	
4.15pm–6.00pm		
6.15pm	Lock up Setting closed	

KS17. Now work out the range of temperatures for each room and find the middle value of each. (The middle value is called the median.) K.Skill N1 2 1c

KS18. Look at the same list of numbers and find out which number occurs most frequently in each room (this number is the mode). Show all your working out. K.Skill N1 2 1c

KS19. Convert the average temperature from degrees Celsius to degrees Fahrenheit. K.Skill N1 2 1b

KS20. You need to encourage children to develop good personal hygiene. Design two pictures (with words) that would help children aged approximately 3 years to learn about personal hygiene. NVQ 202 1 7; K.Skill C1 1 1

KS21. Draw the wall in your bathroom to scale at 4 metres long. At equal distances along the 4 metres, position your pictures (state the measurement in centimetres and millimetres). K.Skill N1 2 1b

KS22. The children travel to school by a variety of different means. These are shown in Figure 3. State which is the most popular method of travel.

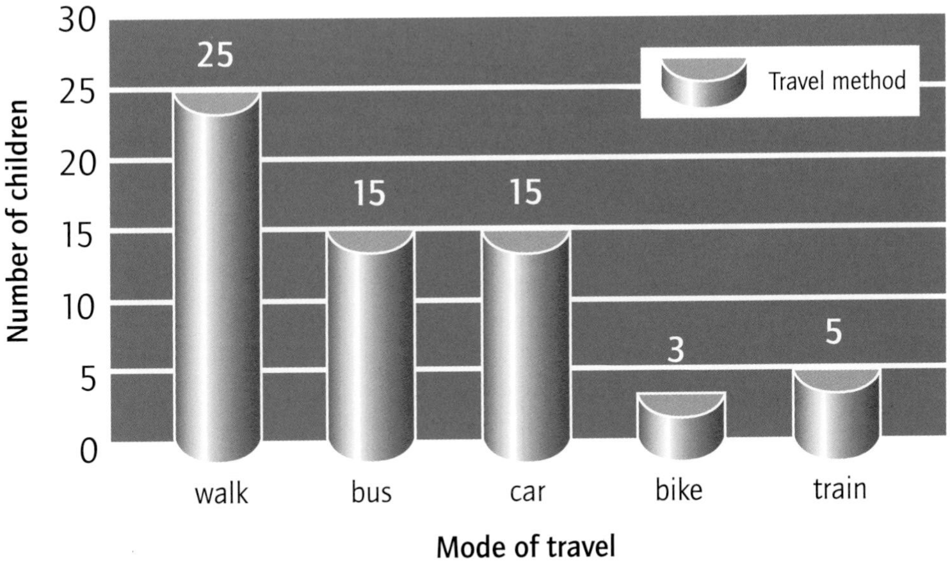

Figure 3: Travel means to Anytown Childcare Centre

KS23. What percentage of all the children walk to school? K.Skill N1 2 1a

KS24. Carry out a survey in your childcare setting to find out how each of the children travel to the setting.

Add up each of the travel methods and draw a bar chart to show your answer. Enter your survey form and all workings out as evidence. K.Skill N1 3 2 3

KS25. Anytown Childcare Centre allows you a weekly budget of £20 to buy incidentals for all the staff and children. Your local shop sells the following:

K.Skill N1 1 — 1

Milk	64p	Sugar	83p	Jam	£1.29
Tea	£3.54	Tissues	£2.10	Marmite	£1.98
Butter	£1.20	Bread	79p	Apples	9p each
Coffee	£2.54				

This week you have bought:

1 Coffee, 5 Milk, 1 Jam, 2 Butter, 5 Bread, 15 Apples and 1 Tissues.

Based on the prices at the corner shop, estimate how much you have spent. Show your working out. Add up the true cost of the items and compare with your estimate.

K.Skill N1 2 — 1c 2

Show all working out in your portfolio.

KS26. During the last eight weeks there have been many observations carried out (see Figure 4 below.)

K.Skill N1 1 2

Add together the number of observations and divide by 63 (the number of children who are currently registered in Anytown Childcare Centre).

Written/narrative	No.
Structured recording	17
Unstructured spontaneous	6
Child study	3
Diaries	25
Snapshots	31
Checklists	**No.**
Precoded checklist	16
Centre-designed checklist	21
Diagrammatic	**No.**
Pie charts	18
Bar charts	18
Sociograms	32
Flow charts	24
Sampling	**No.**
Target child	17
Time sampling	18
Event sampling	19
Total	**265**

Figure 4: Observation techniques

KS27. How many observations, on average, has each child had in the last eight weeks?

KS28. How many observations, on average, has each child had in the last two weeks?

KS29. How many observations will each child have in the next 24 weeks?

K.Skill N1 2 1

Remember to show your working out.

	Number of children who are male	Children who attend full-time	Children who attend part-time	Children who have sibling at centre	Children with allergies	Children that drink milk	Children who do not have English as their first language	Children who have attended more than 1 year	Children who pay fees indep-endently	Children who are paid for by local authority	Children who left owing fees
2000	53	35	65	15	6	57	10	33	35	54	15
2001	49	36	61	12	7	60	17	34	38	53	17
2002	45	40	57	13	9	59	19	35	40	54	12
2003	56	35	63	17	12	61	16	36	45	54	14
2004	54	38	68	10	14	63	19	38	47	55	9
2005	67	42	45	11	16	60	14	39	49	53	9

Note: Anytown Childcare Centre is registered for 63 children. There are 100 names on the register.

Figure 5: Information regarding children at Anytown Childcare Centre

Figure 5 (page 64) shows the statistics that have been gathered together for Anytown Childcare Centre. Answer the following questions showing all your working out. Check your answers (show working out) and transfer as necessary to your Key Skill log book.

KS30. Which year had the most names on the register?

K.Skill N1 2 1

KS31. Work out the average number of children who drank milk from 2002 to 2005 inclusive.

K.Skill N1 2 1

Milk is needed for strong bones and teeth. Record:

NVQ 205 K2H84

- how children's teeth develop
- daily care of teeth required
- effects of poor diet on teeth.

KS32. How many children (families) left owing fees during the six years?

K.Skill N1 2 1

KS33. If each family left owing £753, how much was owed to Anytown Childcare Centre at the end of 2005?

K.Skill N1 2 1

KS34. What do you notice about the number of children with allergies?

K.Skill N1 2 1

KS35. In 2003, how many children (in percentage) attended full-time and how many attended part-time? (Remember to round your answers up or down to the nearest whole number.)

K.Skill N1 2 1

KS36. How does this compare to 2005?

K.Skill N1 2 1

KS37. Write the number of siblings at the centre in words over the six years.

K.Skill N1 1 1

Activity 2.4 Technical Certificate Unit 003 Task Bi

T.Cert 003 Task B i

Before you plan and prepare observations, complete this Technical Certificate Assignment which will assist you in planning activities for developmental areas of a specific age.

Use templates T05.1–T05.4 to show that you know how a childcare practitioner can contribute to development throughout the different age ranges. Give one example of an activity or interaction that can help support development for each age group.

NVQ 203 K2D48 7
K2D49 7
K2D50 7
K2D51 7

EGM Assignment

TARGET DATE:

Assignment 003 Supporting child and young person development at each age range

T05.1

Task Bi

Age	Physical development	Communication and intellectual development	Social, emotional and behavioural development
0–3 years			

T05.2

Age	Physical development	Communication and intellectual development	Social, emotional and behavioural development
3–7 years			

T05.3

Age	Physical development	Communication and intellectual development	Social, emotional and behavioural development
7–12 years			

T05.4

Age	Physical development	Communication and intellectual development	Social, emotional and behavioural development
12–16 years			

Activity 2.5 Questions 10–14

EGM Questioning

It's time now to check your knowledge with some questions:

Q10) What is meant by 'interconnected holistic development'?

Common Core 2

Q11) Record current legislation regarding confidentiality and data protection.

NVQ 208 K2M119

Q12) Why is it necessary to carry out formal observations of babies and children?

NVQ 208 K2D113

Q13) Why must you ask permission before carrying out an observation?

NVQ 208 K2D114

Q14) Why is it important to provide children with a warm, safe, secure and encouraging environment and develop a close and loving relationship with them?

NVQ 203 K2D48 1 3

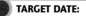

TARGET DATE:

You have now completed Chapter 2. Check with your assessor when your portfolio will be verified. Once an NVQ unit is verified, the certificate can be claimed from the Awarding Body. Check the dates on your Individual Training Plan (ITP), making sure you are on target. Your employer, assessor and training centre will be proud of your progress.

You can now move on to Chapter 3.

3

Observation of children's developmental areas

Chapter contents

Index to activities in Chapter 3

You are now ready to start observing children. You know the sequence of their development and you are familiar with the structure and value of play. The basics of health and safety are well known to you; you have read the policies and procedures of your setting and know how to carry out risk assesments.

So, you are ready. What's stopping you? – let's go!

You can gather the evidence for Unit 203 through many other units (especially Units 206 and 208) but one of the most important skills for you to learn (and one that needs lots of practice) is child observation. By using Unit 203 as your core unit, you can dip in and out of the other units and elements several times but in different ways.

Hints & Tips

Before you begin any activities or tasks remember to read through the whole chapter first.

You are nearly ready to start observing children, but first, let's check you remember the techniques or formats of recording.

Activity 3.1 Technical Certificate Unit 003 Task Aii

T.Cert 003 Task A ii

Common Core 2

Outcomes Framework 1,2,3

List three different ways in which a childcare practitioner can observe and record children and young people's pattern of development.

Activity 3.2 Technical Certificate Unit 003 Task Aiii

T.Cert 003 Task A iii

NVQ 203 K2D41

EGM Questioning

TARGET DATE:

What should you do if you have any concerns about a child or young person's development following an observation?

Observations

The following pages have been broken down into small activities which are referenced Action Plan A or Action Plan B.

- Action Plan A will allow you and the children to practise activities for a developmental area.
- Action Plan B will allow you to observe the children, focusing on the same activities as well as some variations that will support and modify or extend the children's development and learning.

NVQ 203 1,2,3

This means you will be able to carry out observations on each area of development (or as many as you need). You can organise these observations whichever way suits you, your assessor and your setting best; you can carry out several observations in one day, one week or over several days/weeks. The success of these observations will depend on how well you action-plan the activities and use the appropriate recording documents.

Your observations may focus on one child, two children, a small group or a large group. You need to plan this with your assessor.

As you become proficient at observing, you will notice more than one skill at once; for example, you may plan to observe the fine motor skills of a child who is posting different shapes into a box but you may also observe his hand/eye co-ordination and developing intellectual skills.

When you feel confident to integrate one, two or three observations at the same time, speak to your assessor and plan it together. Remember that either your room leader or line manager must also be consulted.

K.Skill Com C1.3 1–3

Start by planning the dates of all the observations on an action plan (keep action plans in a folder).

NVQ 203 1 4

Agree these dates with your assessor and line manager/room leader, allowing time for the children to practise and improve their skills first.

Activity 3.3 Action plan

EGM Work Product
EGM Action Plan
NVQ 203 4
TARGET DATE:

State the age of the children you are working with.

Create an action plan of all areas of development that you want to observe, to support your work in NVQ Element 203.4.

NVQ Unit	Element & PC	Activity			Knowledge Understanding Evidence	Principles & Values Key Skills C.Core
		Areas of development	Practice Date	Completion Date		
203	1. pc 1–4	Physical				
		Gross Motor	16th June	19th June		
		Fine Motor	23rd June			
		Hand/eye	30th June			
		Social & Emotional	7th July			
		Language & Communication	14th July			
		Intellectual	21st July			

Figure 6: An example of an action plan

You can now prepare each observation by completing one action plan for each developmental area.

Action Plan A

On this action plan, record all the activities that you intend to set out for the children. After the children have practised the activities, you may decide to add or take away some of the equipment/resources. Next, adjust and extend action plan A into action plan B by using different coloured inks.

For example: you design an action plan for children to practise their gross motor skills. Your monitoring of their abilities is your first observation. From this, you may add or remove some equipment. On your action plan in a different colour, show what you have added or removed; this is your second observation.

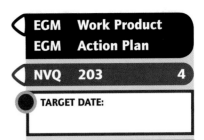

<table>
<tr><th colspan="2">NVQ</th><th colspan="3" rowspan="2">Activity</th><th rowspan="2">Knowledge
Understanding
Evidence</th><th rowspan="2">Principles &
Values
Key Skills
C.Core
Outcomes</th></tr>
<tr><th>Unit</th><th>Element & PC</th></tr>
<tr><td></td><td></td><td>Areas of development

Physical

Gross Motor
Children aged 2–3 years</td><td>Practice Date

16th June</td><td>Completion Date

19th June</td><td></td><td></td></tr>
<tr><td>203</td><td>1. pc 1–4</td><td colspan="3">ACTION PLAN A Practice Day 16th June

• Use large toy room and garden ✓
• Set out equipment for 8 children ✓
• Ask Mary, Room Leader, to help
• In garden put ~~climbing frame (Large)~~ tunnels, bikes, prams, buses, table & chairs for drinks and snacks. Add small climbing frame
• In large play room put buses, scoot-a-longs, hoops, skipping ropes, bean bags. Add stepping blocks, soft balls.

ACTION PLAN B Observation Day 19th June

1. Ask Jane to help Mary whilst I observe.
2. Children will be code names of TC1 and TC2</td><td>K2D48</td><td>Outcomes 123
C Core 2
P&V
P 1.2.
V 1. 3. 4. 5. 6. 9.</td></tr>
</table>

Figure 7: An example of Action Plan A being adjusted to become Action Plan B

Performance criteria

The next few pages are crib sheets. They list the performance criteria that must be met at each observation. You need these so that you can set up, carry out and analyse good observations.

Crib sheet 1 reminds you how to contribute to children's fun.

Crib sheet 2 reminds you what to do before carrying out an observation.

Crib sheet 3 reminds you what to look for during an observation.

Crib sheet 4 is a checklist for general or anecdotal observations.

Crib sheet 1

EGM Direct Observation

This crib sheet tells you how the professional childcare practitioner personally contributes to children's fun and learning.

Common Core 1,2

Principles and Values

These pointers are all performance criteria. They contribute to supporting the child's enjoyment of the activity and his or her social and emotional development. As the childcare practitioner, you must include all these criteria in your everyday work with children.

- Provide a positive and encouraging environment. — **NVQ 203 2 6**
- Ensure your own behaviour is respectful, courteous and appropriate towards children at all times.
- Encourage children to make choices and take decisions for themselves. — **NVQ 202 4 6; NVQ 203 2 5; NVQ 202 4 3**
- Support children's positive behaviour according to the procedures of the setting. — **NVQ 203 2 3; NVQ 202 4 1**
- Encourage children's social development in play and everyday activities. — **NVQ 203 2 2**
- Give praise and encouragement according to the age, needs and abilities of the child. — **NVQ 202 4 2; NVQ 203 2 3**
- Make use of opportunities to encourage children's confidence and self-esteem, allowing them to make choices. — **NVQ 203 2 4; NVQ 202 4 3**
- Take time to communicate with children during everyday activities and routines in ways that the child will understand. — **NVQ 201 3 1**
- Handle sensitively children who find it difficult to participate in activities or that show challenging behaviour, according to the policies and procedures of the setting. — **NVQ 202 4 5; NVQ 206 K2D102**
- Work with children to apply rules and boundaries consistently, appropriately and fairly, according to age, needs and abilities. — **NVQ 202 4 4**

Crib sheet 2

This crib sheet reminds you what a professional childcare practitioner will do before carrying out an observation.

Before you start planning the activities on which you will observe the children, read the following hints and tips carefully. (These pointers are all performance criteria.)

EGM Direct Observation

- Always follow the policies and procedures of the setting regarding child observations and the reporting of any concerns about development. *(Always ask permission to read the policies of your setting. It is important that you become familiar with them.)*

NVQ 208 K2D117
NVQ 203 K2D41
Common Core 6

- Remember the importance of confidentiality, data protection and information sharing. *(Never gossip about children, families, colleagues or your setting.)*

NVQ 203 1 2
203 K2M42
203 2 7
5

- Make sure you record the child's exact date of birth and age in years and months. *(Be specific, as a few months in age can make a vast difference in ability.)*

NVQ 207 2 1

- Always record observations of development accurately, using different observation formats. *(Observation is part of your everyday work.)*

NVQ 208 K2D118

- Remember to ask permission of the child (if old enough), the parent and your line manager. *(It is essential to gain a signature for permission.)*

NVQ 208 K2D114

- Work in partnership with a childcare practitioner who will supervise the children whilst you observe their activities.
- Work within the routines of your setting, the curriculum or framework plans.

NVQ 203 K2D48 7

- Give children time to practise their skills before you observe them.
- Ensure your activities are appropriate to the age, ability and needs of children and will allow for the inclusion of all.

NVQ 203 K2D48 2

- Remember to be unobtrusive and sensitive.
- Do not make negative remarks or judgements.
- Understand the purpose of careful observation and note taking of what children do and say and how they behave.

NVQ 203 K2D39

After an observation

NVQ 203 K2D40

Remember the importance of checking your observations of children with colleagues and parents, again according to the policy of your setting, prior to assessment. When you have completed your observation, remember to share and record your findings accurately and in confidence with the appropriate people, based on the procedures and requirements of your setting.

NVQ 208 K2M120
NVQ 203 2 7
1 2
3 5

Crib sheet 3

This crib sheet reminds you what a professional childcare practitioner looks for when observing children. Remember that these pointers are all performance criteria.

Pay careful attention to children, observing how they:

- move around the setting and co-ordinate their movements — NVQ 203 1 1
- make use of space and large equipment
- manipulate and use small equipment
- behave in a group — NVQ 203 K2D39
- assess their own risk in a controlled environment through play — NVQ 206 4 2; NVQ 206 K2D101
- express their feelings and emotions — NVQ 203 2 1
- relate to each other and to adults
- play and use their imagination — NVQ 203 3 1
- concentrate on activities
- memorise things — NVQ 203 3 1
- pay attention to what is around them
- gain new information
- show their creativity
- benefit from play and exercise
- confidently participate in the activity (make use of opportunities to increase their confidence and self-esteem) — NVQ 203 2 4
- communicate verbally or non-verbally with adults and each other — EGM Direct Observation
- use language, including speaking, listening, reading and writing
- respond and participate in language activities.

EGM Direct Observation

Crib sheet 4

EGM **Direct Observation**

This crib sheet is for you to write short or casual observations. The following points serve as memory hooks when you come to record the more detailed observation.

Observe how the children:

- play, noting what they do and how they do it — **NVQ 203 K2D39**
- move round the setting, co-ordinating their movements — **NVQ 203 1 1a**
- manipulate and use small equipment — **NVQ 203 1 1c**
- make use of large muscles — **NVQ 203 1 3a**
- use hand/eye co-ordination — **NVQ 203 1 3c**
- make use of space and large equipment — **NVQ 203 1 1b**
- use small, fine movement muscles — **NVQ 203 1 3b**
- express their feelings and emotions — **NVQ 203 2 1a**
- relate to each other and adults — **NVQ 203 2 1b**
- use play and imagination — **NVQ 203 3 1a**
- concentrate on activities — **NVQ 203 3 1b**
- gain new information — **NVQ 203 3 1e**
- memorise things — **NVQ 203 3 1c**
- show their creativity — **NVQ 203 3 1f**
- pay attention to what is around them — **NVQ 203 3 1d**
- communicate verbally and non-verbally with adults and each other — **NVQ 203 3 3a**
- use language, including speaking, listening, reading and writing — **NVQ 203 3 3b**
- respond and participate in language activities. — **NVQ 203 3 3c**

Remember...

This list is not exhaustive and you may add as many extras as you feel necessary.

To help you record the children's skills, use templates T06.1–T06.2 as many times as you want at each observation.

General anecdotal observations

T06.1

Observation	Child 1 code name	Date	Child 2 code name	Date
How they move round setting, co-ordinating their movements **203 1 1a**				
Use of space and large equipment **203 1 1b**				
How they manipulate and use small equipment **203 1 1c**				
Use of gross motor/large muscles **203 1 3a**				
Use of fine movement/small muscles **203 1 3b**				
Hand/eye co-ordination **203 1 3c**				
How they express feelings and emotions **203 2 1a**				
How they relate to each other and adults **203 2 1b**				
Use of play and imagination **203 3 1a**				

T06.2

Observation	Child 1 code name	Date	Child 2 code name	Date
How they concentrate on activities **203 3 1b**				
How they memorise things **203 3 1c**				
How they pay attention to what is around them **203 3 1d**				
How they gain new information **203 3 1e**				
How they show their creativity **203 3 1f**				
How they communicate verbally and non-verbally with adults and with each other **203 3 3a**				
Use of language, including speaking, listening, reading, writing **203 3 3b**				
How they respond and take part in language opportunities **203 3 3c**				

Hints & Tips

Remember the following points for each observation...

You will need to gain Expert Witness Testimonies when you plan and carry out activities and observations during practise time. There must be direct observations for each element, therefore your assessor will need to observe you carrying out these activities – it is your responsibility to plan this with the assessor, setting the date and time.

Make sure you share and record your findings accurately with the appropriate person in your setting.

Carry out a **risk assessment** before the children take part in the activity. If any hazards are found, show how you have removed or reduced them. Risk assessments must be stored in your portfolio as evidence of your competence, knowledge and skills.

Remember to make an **holistic assessment** for each observation. This means you will be producing one piece of work that may demonstrate evidence for more than one criteria. For example, when planning and carrying out these activities for observations:

- usethe space in the room effectively
- setthe furniture and equipment out so that entrances, exits and fire exits are not blocked and the activities can be carried out safely.

EGM Expert Witness Testimony
EGM Direct Observation

NVQ 203 1 2
2 7
3 5

NVQ 202 1 2
3

EGM Work Product

NVQ 205 1 1–3
NVQ 205 K2D63

Health and Safety

Hints & Tips

A few examples of basic activities are listed for you in front of each development area/activity.

Use the activity number from this book as the reference number for your child observation in your evidence portfolio.

Use the crib sheets with your observations, meeting each performance criteria to ensure that you show evidence of competence.

Whenever possible, use different recording techniques for the different observation aims, being sure to identify activities that support children's play and learning.

Check that your assessor and childcare practioner are still available for direct observations.

For each observation you must set the scene, describing the activities, environment and number of children/adults in the group. You must state which age range you are working with for each activity and observation.

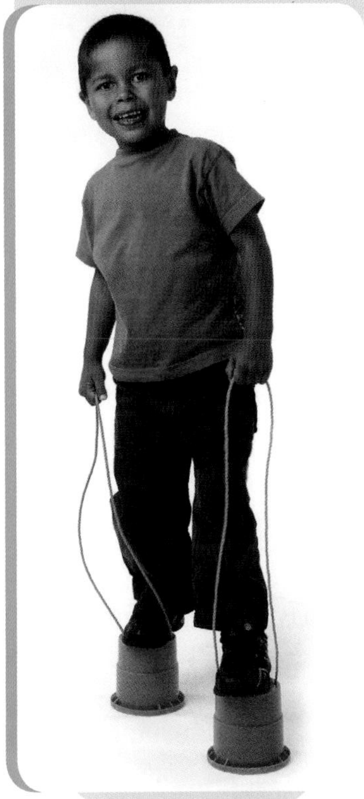

Child observations: gross motor activities

Gross motor activities, or large muscle movements, are essential to the growing child.

You are probably aware from government advertising that eating the right foods in the right proportions is the basis for healthy living (more about this in Chapter 6). However, the development and growth of a healthy body is also dependent upon exercise. Exercise strengthens and develops muscles, so young children should be allowed daily exercise, varying from vigorous to moderate to low activity. This builds up the skills of the large muscles, making them more refined. Activity also improves the circulation of blood around the body, breaks down fatty tissues and contributes to building healthy bones.

NVQ 205 K2D80

Physical exercise for children should be fun, imaginative, varied in its purpose and aimed at different body parts.

As a childcare practitioner, you should try to set up physical activities each day, varying from vigorous to moderate levels of exercise. Remember to encourage all children to participate in the activities.

NVQ 205 3 2

EGM Expert Witness Testimony

Examples of gross motor activities

The following are outline activities only. You can use some of these ideas or make up your own. All of the activities incorporate the whole body.

- Walking, running, jumping, hopping, skipping, crawling, shuffling, rolling, climbing, swimming, kicking
- Being an animal, e.g. frog, kangaroo, elephant, monkey, bird
- Dancing, being a fairy, moving to music
- Games, e.g. Oranges and lemons; Teddy bear, teddy bear; What's the time Mr Wolf?; Round and round the mulberry bush
- Races, e.g. egg and spoon race, sack race
- Using toys, e.g. tractors, bicycles, prams, scooters, cars, lorries, buses
- Using equipment, e.g. climbing frames, tree houses, balancing bars, seesaws, barrels, trampolines, pop-ups, tunnels, ball pools
- Using PE equipment, e.g. gym mats, parachutes, balls, hoops, games, footballs, toddler trampolines.

The following activities are suitable for children over 5 years.

- Games – football, cricket, netball, rounders, any bat and ball game
- Hoops for skipping and spinning round waist
- Playground games, e.g. Hopscotch, It, Bulldog, Jacks
- Stilts, frisbees, batons
- Skateboards
- Roller skates
- Horse riding
- Cycling.

Activity 3.4 Action plan A – gross motor

Common Core 3
Outcomes Framework 2

Use an action plan to help you plan activities that will encourage and support children to take part in **gross motor** development, to take turns and to consider others.

NVQ 206 4 1, 4

Make effective use of the physical space by providing interesting and stimulating opportunities that allow for the use of large equipment, thus encouraging gross motor and whole body movement.

NVQ 205 1 1
NVQ 206 4 3
NVQ 203 1 1b, 3a

An element of risk and challenge should be provided in the children's physical play, to allow them to assess their own risk in play according to their age, ability and needs.

NVQ 206 4 1, 2

Ensure that the environment supports the children's physical skills, promoting their confidence in movement.

NVQ 203 K2D48 17

Before you prepare to observe, give the children time and opportunity to practise their physical skills, move around the setting and co-ordinate their movements.

NVQ 203 1 1a, 4

Gain an expert witness testimony, recording the activities you carried out and stating how they supported the developmental areas of the children and related to the framework or curriculum theme in your setting.

EGM Expert Witness Testimony
EGM Action Plan

TARGET DATE:

Activity 3.5 Action Plan B – gross motor

Adjust Action Plan A activities for gross motor development by either adding or taking away equipment, materials and other resources, to modify or extend the level of activity.

Carry out your observation on gross motor development.

EGM **Direct Observation**
EGM **Child Observation**

When you have completed your observation on gross motor development, read your observation again and reflect on your work.

EGM **Reflective Account**

DON'T FORGET

Each unit has a list of knowledge specifications relevant to its elements. Competent performance is dependent upon you demonstrating the knowledge through the activity.

TARGET DATE:

Activity 3.6 Questions 15–19

EGM **Questioning**

Q15) Which recording format or technique did you use for observation of gross motor activities? Why did you choose this method?

Q16) What health and safety points did you consider when setting out the equipment in the environment?

Q17) How did you follow the equal opportunities and inclusion policy of your setting?

Q18) Which of the values did you work within?

Q19) How did you supervise the children's safety, adjusting your approach according to their age, needs and abilities?

Health and Safety

Principles and Values

NVQ 202 K2H26
NVQ 206 4 6

TARGET DATE:

Activity 3.7 Professional discussion

Make an appointment with your assessor to have an in-depth discussion on the work you have completed.

Use the feedback to find out which areas of your work (both the activities and observations) need further development.

NVQ 204 1 4
NVQ 204 K2P52

EGM Professional Discussion

TARGET DATE:

Child observations: fine motor activities

For a child, the majority of fine motor movements are co-ordinated by hand and eye control. This is a complex skill as the child learns to co-ordinate the use of fine motor muscles in the hands and fingers at the same time as focusing his or her eye on the activity. For example, grasping a crayon then making a mark on the paper, holding a cube and trying to post it through a posting box or threading a bead.

The development of fine motor muscles in the hands and fingers allows the child to manipulate objects such as tools for woodwork and clay modelling, pens for writing and drawing, brushes for painting pictures and needles for sewing.

As a childcare practitioner, you can help children develop fine motor skills and hand/eye co-ordination by the careful selection of activities.

Examples of fine motor activities

- Jigsaws, posting boxes, beads and string, inset boards
- Zips, buttons, hooks and eyes, laces
- Paper sticking, weaving, threading
- Eating using a knife, fork, spoon; drinking using a cup
- Construction toys of all sorts
- Small-world role play, e.g. dressing dolls, farms, airports, garage
- Sand/water play, pouring, digging, building, using a computer mouse.

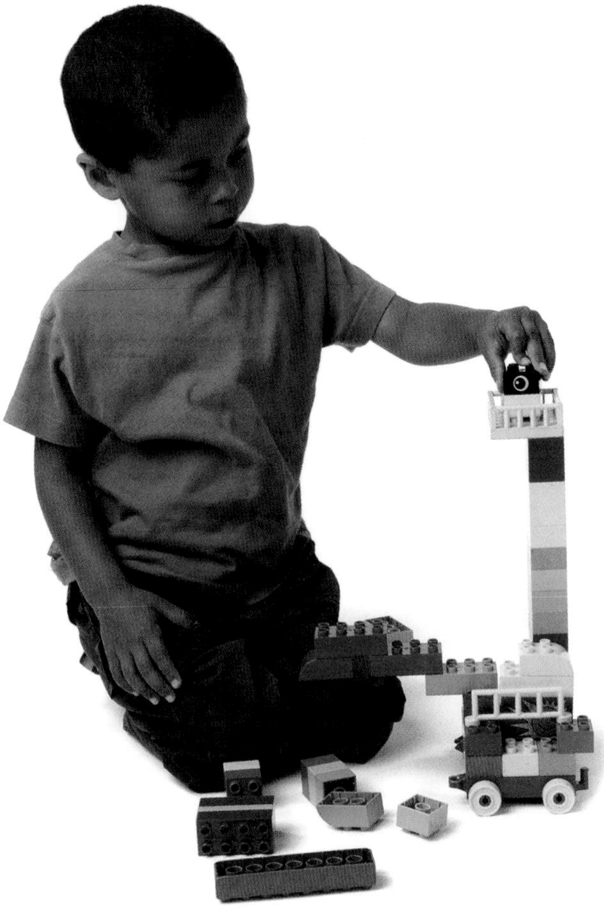

Examples of creative play

- All arts and crafts, including the many ways of painting, crayoning, drawing, modelling, making collages, using different colours and textures and working with natural and synthetic materials
- Working on different types of paper, card and board
- Using paint with additives, e.g. washing powder
- Glueing, cutting, sticking
- Dancing, music movement, creating an individual style
- Drama and role play, dressing up
- Sand play – wet, dry, with shells, stones, diggers, dinosaurs, etc.
- Water – warm, cold, with ice, bubbles, colours, perfumes, items for sinking, floating, filling, pouring.

Activity 3.8 Action Plan A – fine motor

Common Core 3
Outcomes Framework 2
NVQ 203 1 3c 3b
NVQ 203 K2D48 9

Use an action plan to help you plan activities that will encourage and support children to take part in **fine motor** activities. State the equipment, materials and resources you will be using, both indoors and out, for the age, needs and abilities of your group.

NVQ 203 K2D48 8

Make sure the materials will encourage the children to explore, investigate and manipulate.

NVQ 203 K2D48 7
NVQ 206 4 5

Allow the children to take part in practice activities as part of their daily routine, giving them time to adjust to the fine motor skills required before you observe them.

NVQ 203 K2D48 11

Encourage their creative play by praise, suggestions and extension of ideas.

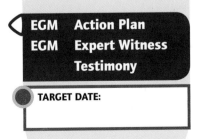

EGM Action Plan
EGM Expert Witness Testimony

Gain an expert witness testimony, recording the activities you carried out and stating how they supported the development areas of the children and related to the framework or curriculum theme in your setting.

TARGET DATE:

Activity 3.9 Action Plan B – fine motor

Adjust Action Plan A activities for **fine motor** development by either adding or taking away equipment, materials and other resources, to modify or extend the level of activity.

Carry out your observation on fine motor development.

When you have completed your observation on fine motor development, read your observation again and reflect on your work.

NVQ 203 1 1c

EGM Action Plan

EGM Direct Observation
EGM Child Observation

EGM Reflective Account

DON'T FORGET

Each unit has a list of knowledge specifications relevant to its elements. Competent performance is dependent upon your demonstrating the knowledge through the activity.

TARGET DATE:

Activity 3.10 Questions 20–26

EGM Questioning

Q20) What health and safety issues did you consider when setting up the activities?

Q21) How did you encourage children to be aware of personal safety and the safety of others?

NVQ 202 1 6

Q22) When did you praise and encourage children?

NVQ 202 4 2

Q23) How did you check that all equipment and materials were appropriate for the age and ability of the children?

Q24) Draw a plan of your environment showing the position of all equipment. How would you have adapted this room for a child with disabilities or special educational needs?

Q25) How did you use everyday care routines to support the activities?

Q26) How did you help children to recognise their own achievements?

NVQ 202 K2D22

NVQ 203 K2D48 7

NVQ 205 3 3

TARGET DATE:

Activity 3.11 Reflective account

Reflect back on your work and the activities for fine motor development.

Record your thoughts, using reflective strategies to analyse your performance.

EGM Reflective Account

Store all the child observations of physical activities together, ensuring that each one is written clearly and is without spelling or punctuation mistakes.

K.Skill Com C1.3 1–3

TARGET DATE:

Child observations: emotional and social development

For children to be emotionally satisfied and socially balanced, a mixture of their needs must be met. Children depend for balanced growth and development on love and security, close bonded relationships, new experiences, trust, praise and recognition.

As a childcare practitioner, you must aim to meet the emotional and social needs of the child in partnership with his or her parents/guardians.

Children need to become aware of themselves and their feelings, and start to value themselves and feel valued by their friends and carers. Each young child needs to have one key person who cares for him or her in the childcare setting. This key person should address all of the child's personal needs, give him or her cuddles and role play desirable behaviour to the group.

As a childcare practitioner, you can support and promote children's social and emotional development by setting a variety of activities that both promote sharing and are competitive (with a winner). Role play and imaginative games allow children to go outside themselves and feel what it is like to be someone else.

Examples of emotional and social development activities

- Games – paired, group, competitive
- Activities where the children share, take turns, show respect to each other, help each other
- Small-world play, e.g. farms, garages, dolls houses; role play of adult
- Role-play activities, e.g. dressing up, camping, shop play, hospitals, doctors and nurses
- Table activities such as construction toys, sticking, glueing, cutting, cooking, play dough, meal times
- Cultural artefacts and costumes
- Stories with/without props
- Drama, e.g. acting of stories, nursery rhymes

Activity 3.12 Action Plan A – emotional and social

EGM Action Plan

Use an action plan to help you plan activities that will encourage and support the children to take part in **emotional and social** activities. Ensure that some of the activities will encourage children to make choices and take decisions.

NVQ 201 3 3
NVQ 203 2 2
5

Allow the children to practise these activities, helping them to cope positively with their feelings and encouraging their emotional well-being. Play with and alongside the children, sensitively supporting their play.

NVQ 203 K2D48 4
12

Be supportive in your response to children's behaviour, following the policies of the setting.

NVQ 203 K2D48 6

Make sure all the activities remain within the daily routine of the setting, allowing time for any toilet training, hand washing, drinks, meals and snacks.

NVQ 203 K2D48 5

Record activities that will allow children to relate to each other and express their feelings. Ensure the environment is positive and encouraging and that the routine allows for children to have quiet periods.

NVQ 203 2 2
1
6
NVQ 203 K2D48 13

Carry out the observations, making sure the environment remains safe and positive, allowing the children to make choices and decisions for themselves.

NVQ 203 K2D48 4
NVQ 205 1 5
NVQ 205 K2D61

Gain an expert witness testimony, recording the activities you carried out and stating how these supported the development areas of the children and related to the framework or curriculum theme in your setting.

EGM Expert Witness Testimony

TARGET DATE:

Activity 3.13 Action Plan B – emotional and social

Adjust Action Plan A activities for **emotional and social** development by either adding or taking away equipment, materials and other resources, to modify or extend the level of activity.

Carry out your observation on emotional and social development.

NVQ 203 1 1c

EGM Action Plan

EGM Direct Observation

EGM Child Observation

Remember that children will play out roles they see at home and in the world around them. Deal sensitively with different behaviours.

NVQ 206 K2D95

When you have completed your observation on social and emotional development, read your observation again and reflect on your work.

EGM Reflective Account

DON'T FORGET

Each unit has a list of knowledge specifications relevant to its elements. Competent performance is dependent upon you demonstrating the knowledge through the activity.

TARGET DATE:

Activity 3.14 Questions 27–30

Q27) Why is it important to give all children in the group the opportunity to express their points of view/feelings?

NVQ 201 K2C2

Q28) Why is it important that children make choices? How can you help children to do this?

NVQ 201 K2D5

Q29) Give examples of how children's behaviour can denote illness.

NVQ 202 2 5

NVQ 202 K2H38

Q30) If you wanted to take the children on an outing, what are the safety issues you would have to consider?

TARGET DATE:

Activity 3.15 Professional discussion

Make an appointment with your assessor to have an in-depth discussion on the work you have completed.

Use the feedback to find out which areas of your work (both activities and observations) need further development.

NVQ 204 2 5

EGM Professional Discussion

TARGET DATE:

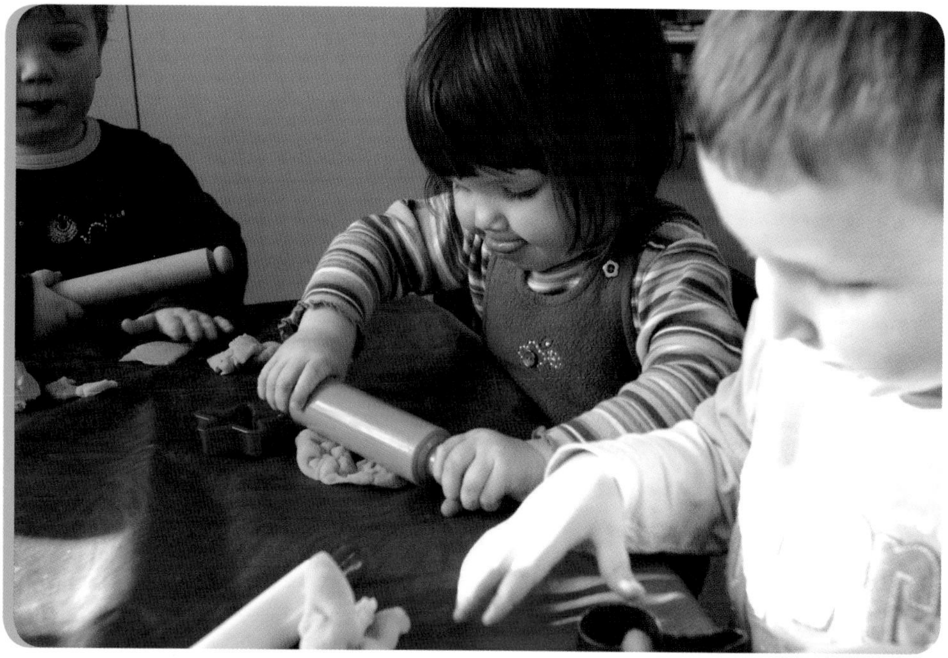

Child observations: language and communication

It can be argued that humans are superior to animals because they have the power of speech. How sad, then, that people do not always use it to its best and fullest advantage.

The baby who gives an involuntary cry at birth is starting on a long road to language acquistion. At first, babies only have pre-verbal communication, but you should talk to them at all times of personal interaction. This allows them to start making sense of the words you use and other vocal sounds. Babies need lots of help and you, as the childcare practitioner, must be there to give support. Gradually, through love, patience and teaching, toddlers learn to speak. They gain an understanding of language and how to express themselves. They talk to themselves at play and, with maturity, they have conversations with their friends, family and peers.

Examples of language and communication activities

- Stories – reading, using props, using no book and no props (made-up or well-known stories)
- Books with words/without words; fiction, non-fiction; books with positive images of disabilities, different cultures, religions, emotions, behaviours, fear/worry
- Songs and rhymes
- Stories – learning new words, picture word boards, pictures
- Talking, listening, questions, praise, recall, exchange of information, labelling, describing, predicting, negotiating
- Games, e.g. memory, smells, taste, matching pairs, families, feely bags
- Hearing – tapes, music, songs.

Activity 3.16 Action Plan A – language and communication

EGM Action Plan

Outcomes Framework 2

NVQ 203 3 4

Use an action plan to help you plan activities that will encourage and support children to take part in **language and communication** activities. State the equipment, materials and resources you will be using, both indoors and out, for the age, needs and abilities of your group.

NVQ 203 3 1a-f 2

Give the children a good variety of activities that will allow them to communicate, memorise and gain new information, show their creativity and pay attention to what is around them.

NVQ 206 K2D90

Songs, music and movement, and games also promote language development.

As the childcare practitioner, you should observe how children:

- communicate verbally and non-verbally
- watch and listen
- pause, taking turns in making sounds or conversation (NVQ 203 K2D48 14)
- make eye contact
- use body language and gestures. (NVQ 203 3 3a-c)

You should encourage children's language development by: (NVQ 206 K2D92)

- asking open-ended questions
- extending their learning by use of appropriate language

- asking for recall of happenings and events
- using prediction to help them think of 'what if'
- exchanging information.

Gain an expert witness testimony, recording the activities you carried out and stating how they supported the development areas of the children and related to the framework or curriculum theme in your setting.

EGM **Expert Witness Testimony**

TARGET DATE:

Activity 3.17 Action Plan B – language and communication

Adjust Action Plan A activities for **language and communication** development by either adding or taking away equipment, materials and other resources, to modify or extend the level of activity.

EGM **Action Plan**

Carry out your observation on language and communication development, paying attention to the way the children:

EGM **Direct Observation**

NVQ **203 K2D48** **14**

- use language
- talk
- listen
- read
- write
- take turns
- take in sounds and conversation
- make eye contact
- sing songs and rhymes
- listen to stories
- exhibit negative behaviour.

NVQ **208 4** **9**

When you have completed your observation on language and communication development, read your observation again and reflect on your work.

EGM **Reflective Account**

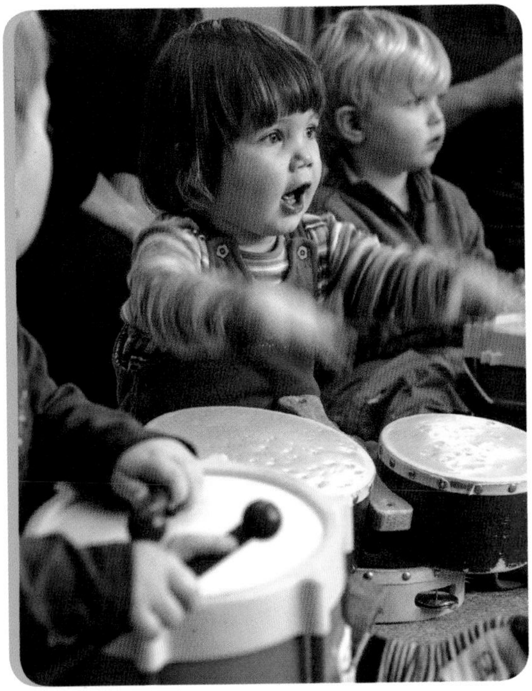

DON'T FORGET

Each unit has a list of knowledge specifications relevant to its elements. Competent performance is dependent upon you demonstrating the knowledge through the activity

TARGET DATE:

Activity 3.18 Questions 31–36

Q31) If your setting was multilingual or bilingual, how would you support children's early communication and intellectual development and learning? Record the activities you would use and why.

NVQ 203 K2D48 15
NVQ 206 K2D85

Q32) How did you ensure all the children took part in the activities equally?

NVQ 203 K2D48 2

Q33) Describe the different ways children have used communication to strengthen relationships.

NVQ 203 K2D48 14

Q34) How did you help children to express their feelings, especially if any were cross or frustrated?

NVQ 203 K2D48 6

Q35) Explain why it is important to give children sufficient time to express themselves.

NVQ 201 1 3
NVQ 201 K2C4

Q36) Give examples of times when you have encouraged children to use different communication methods, stating the reasons why.

NVQ 201 3 5
NVQ 208 4 8

Activity 3.19 Reflective account

Reflect back on your work and the activities for fine motor development. Record your thoughts using reflective strategies to analyse your performance.

NVQ 204 2 5
NVQ 204 K2P58
NVQ 207 1 5

EGM Reflective Account

TARGET DATE:

Child observations: intellectual development

Intellectual development is the development of the part of the brain that thinks, reasons and understands. As a baby's five senses mature, so he or she learns by seeing, hearing, smelling, tasting and touching.

All children are born with natural intelligence, genes that are inherited from their parents. However, intellectual development can be encouraged or nurtured by stimulating a child's mind from a young age. It is therefore important that you, as the childcare practitioner, know the sequence of intellectual development and plan activities for children according to their needs and abilities. You must provide lots of opportunities for them to learn, giving them plenty of support and encouragement and helping them to understand in an exciting, inspirational environment.

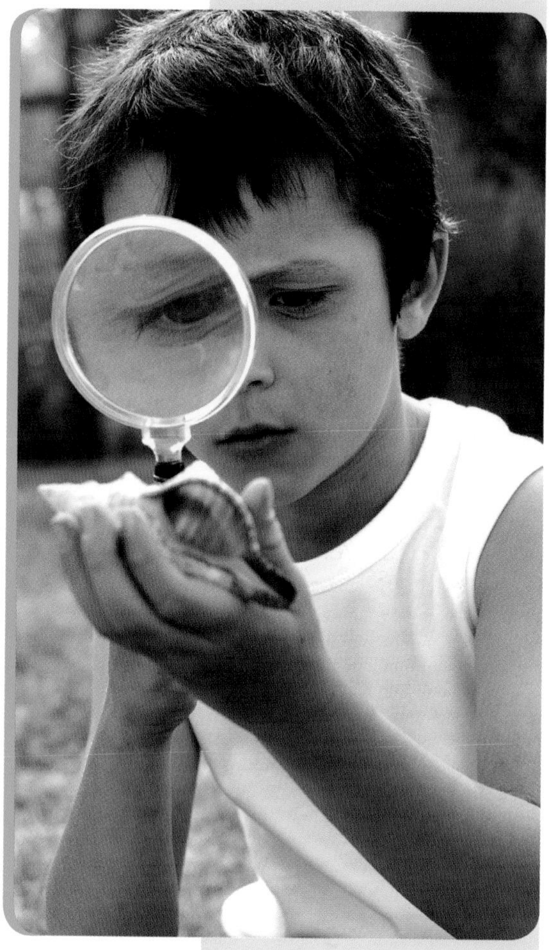

Examples of intellectual development activities

Activities to promote intellectual development are integrated within all the other activities you give children, but you also need to give them activities that will extend their concentration and develop their understanding of quantity, time and number, etc. Examples of activities to encourage children's intellectual development include:

- understanding celebrations of birthday, Christmas, Eid, etc.
- developing memory skills so they can understand past, present and future
- recognising familiar happenings and routines, so these start to have meaning
- exploring, sorting, and investigating activities
- developing number, letter and word recognition (understanding of the world around them)
- developing an interest in ICT and technological toys
- learning about geography, history and science, so these start to have meaning.

Activity 3.20 Action Plan A – intellectual development

EGM Action Plan

Outcomes Framework 2

NVQ 203 3 2

Use an action plan to help you plan activities that will encourage and support children's **intellectual** development, according to their needs and abilities. Let them practise and make mistakes, but be ready to help them as necessary.

Pay careful attention to the children, noting how they:

NVQ 203 3 1

- concentrate on activities
- pay attention to what is around them
- gain new information
- use play and imagination
- show their creativity
- memorise things.

Ensure you support children's interest in numbers, counting, sorting, matching, early reading and mark-making.

NVQ 203 K2D48 10 16

Common Core 1, 2

Gain an expert witness testimony, recording the activities you carried out and stating how they supported the developmental areas of the children and related to the framework or curriculum theme in your setting.

EGM Expert Witness Testimony

TARGET DATE:

Activity 3.21 Action Plan B – intellectual development

Adjust Action Plan A activities for **intellectual** development by either adding or taking away equipment, materials and other resources, to modify or extend the level of activity.

EGM Action Plan

Carry out your observation on intellectual development.

EGM Direct Observation

When you have completed your observation on intellectual development, read your observation again and reflect on your work.

EGM Reflective Account

DON'T FORGET

Each unit has a list of knowledge specifications relevant to its elements. Competent performance is dependent upon you demonstrating the knowledge through the activity.

Whilst reflecting on the activities you set out for the children, answer the following:

Q37) Having completed several observations, write a reflective narrative explaining what you have gained from the observations and how you have been able to extend the children's learning.

Q38) Discuss the strengths and weaknesses of your personal practice and how these are affected by your own background and experiences.

NVQ 204 K2P52
K2P53
NVQ 207 K207H09

Activity 3.22 Professional discussion

Make an appointment with your assessor to have an in-depth discussion on the work you have completed. Use the feedback to find out which areas of your work (both activities and observations) need further development.

NVQ 204 2 5
EGM Professional Discussion
TARGET DATE:

You have now completed observations on children's different areas of development. Consider carefully what you have found out about children through your observations.

Activity 3.23 Questions 39–46

Q39) How will the findings of the observation help you with the assessment and planning for children?

NVQ 203 4 1

Plan with your room leader how you are going to participate in the assessment of children's development.

NVQ 203 4 2

Q40) Who will you discuss these observations with and why?

Q41) How did you personally contribute ideas and suggestions to the assessment of support planning for the child's development?

NVQ 203 4 3

Q42) Which techniques did you use for observing the children in relation to each developmental area?

Q43) Why did you choose these techniques?

Q44) Explain why you designed the observation format you used in at least one observation.

Gain an expert witness testimony stating how you contributed ideas and suggestions towards planning for children in your setting.

EGM Expert Witness Testimony

Q45) Write a list of records that must be kept on the children in your care.

Q46) With whom would you share these records, according to the policies and procedures of your setting?

NVQ 207 K207H03
TARGET DATE:

Activity 3.24 Technical Certificate Unit 003 Task Bii

T.Cert 003 B ii

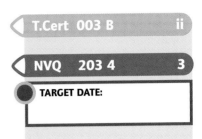

NVQ 203 4 3

TARGET DATE:

Why is it important to plan appropriate activities for children and young people's learning and development, and how can the childcare practitioner contribute to planning?

You have now nearly completed Chapter 3 on your holistic journey through the apprenticeship framework for Children's Care, Learning and Development.

You need to think about children from their earliest stage of infancy to being a teenager at 16 years of age. On this journey they will pass from one stage to another, from one state to another, and from one place to another.

Show your understanding of the transitions in a child's life by completing the last two tasks of the Technical Certificate.

Activity 3.25 Technical Certificate Unit 003 Task Biii

T.Cert 003 Task B iii

NVQ 203 K2T112

TARGET DATE:

Although every person is unique, there are many similarities in what happens to children and young people in life. Draw a picture, for example, a life 'snake'. Identify on it the significant transitions that may happen throughout a child/young person's life between birth and 16 years of age.

Activity 3.26 Technical Certificate Unit 003 Task Biv

T.Cert 003 Task B iv

Briefly explain how a childcare practitioner can support children and young people through each transition you have identified.

TARGET DATE:

Finally, have you remembered to complete Technical Certificate Task A (Principles and Values) on your journey through the last two chapters?

Give all your work a final check, cross-referencing it where necessary.

If you have completed all the activities and assignments, then you have completed Unit 203, Technical Certificate 003, and Communication and Application of Number Key Skills.

Keep going – Chapter 4 is exciting!

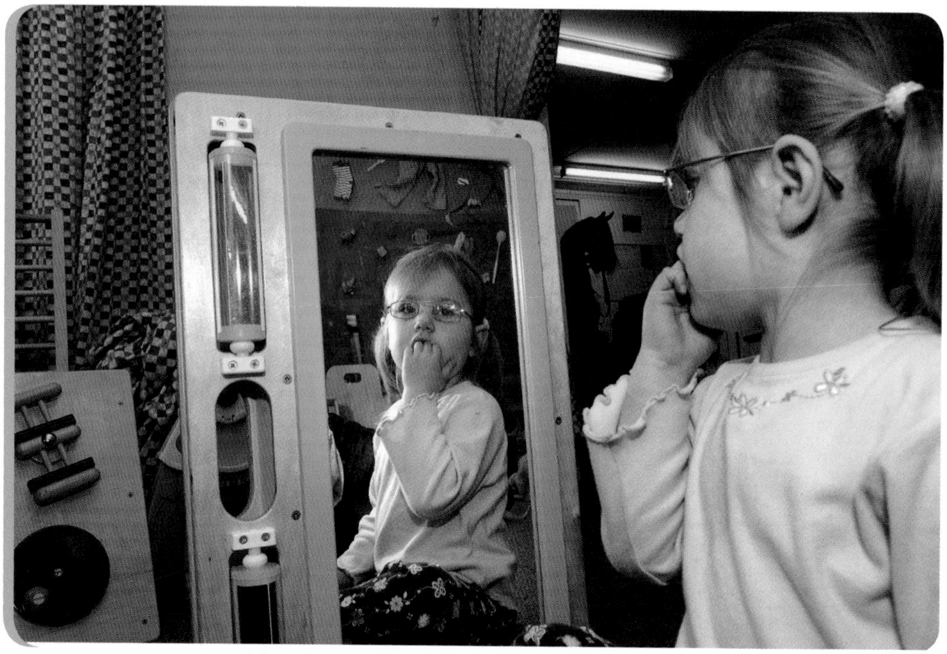

4

Preparing environments to support children's play and learning

Chapter contents

Index to activities in Chapter 4

The environment

Outcomes Framework 1,2

Common Core 1,2,3

You are moving on now to preparing environments for children. Quite rightly many of you will feel that you have already set up a variety of environments, but when you did this your main focus was on child observation.

The experienced childcare practitioner would have had both the child observation and the environment as a joint focus, but as you are learning, it is better for you to take one focus at a time.

The environment plays a very important part in promoting and supporting the development of children.

Think of your room at home. If it is disorganised and messy, you may feel disheartened and as though you can't be bothered. If, however, it is clean and tidy and has some of your favourite bits and pieces neatly displayed, you may feel happy, ready to relax, work or play.

If you relate this to an environment for children, you can quickly see how important it is that the environment is set up to stimulate play, learning and other activities. But above all, it must be safe.

Common Core 2

NVQ 205 K2D62

The environment is everywhere that you work and care for children – a room, a hall, a school, a sleep room, a bathroom, a garden or a playground. Wherever it is, it must be safe, stimulating, exciting and suitable for everyone, whether able-bodied or disabled. It must display positive images of young and old, from different cultures, ethnicities and genders.

This next chapter of your learning journey will help you learn how to set up stimulating environments to encourage children to explore, create and investigate.

Developing a stimulating and learning environment

All environments must share some basic similarities. They must be clean and tidy, and conform to health and safety requirements. They must be inviting and stimulating for children. There should be an array of different textures and vibrant colours. The environment must be maintained and items replenished as used.

Natural and synthetic materials should be evident. There should be different learning areas, relevant for children from birth to early learning goals. To help you set up environments, keep quiet areas together, away from messy and noisy activities. Ensure that children can reach all the resources and that they are clearly labelled with pictures and words.

Remember, the environment means indoors and outdoors, and should extend to bathrooms, sleep and other areas such as corridors, and entrance areas.

To help you build a stimulating learning environment, let's record what you need to include:

- role-play/drama area
- creative art and craft area
- large and small construction toys
- area for small-world play
- music and sound-making items
- area for sand/soil/peat/water play, etc.
- book corner, showing words and pictures
- malleable materials
- problem-solving, reasoning and numeracy area
- growing items and areas
- spaces for large muscle/gross motor development
- wood work area
- ICT and other technological toys.

Crib sheet 5

This crib sheet is for you to use each time you set up an environment.

The following pointers are performance criteria. They all contribute to a safe and stimulating environment. As a childcare practitioner, you must include all these criteria in your everyday work with children.

- Do not block fire exits or doorways on either side.
- Ensure adequate ventilation and heating.
- Check safety of outside area – look for fences, gates, poisonous plants, berries, animal faeces.
- Carry out risk assessments and follow health and safety procedures.
- Use space effectively, position furniture and equipment carefully, and allow children to move freely and safely.
- Ensure the environment caters for all children.
- Make the environment inviting and stimulating.
- Consider how you will build your environment, inside and out.
- Make it possible for children to celebrate their own culture within your environment and encourage children to socialise with each other and adults.
- Provide different shaped and sized objects that will promote physical development.
- Use objects that can be grouped together by size, colour, type, feel, shape, etc. for further learning.
- Offer light and heavy objects made from natural and synthetic materials.
- Use objects and items that will engage children's different interests and needs.
- Use equipment safely, conforming to manufacturers' instructions and setting requirements.
- Help children to make progress with their development according to their age, needs and abilities.
- Help children to express their needs and make choices.
- Set up ICT and help children to use it as part of their exploration and investigation skills.
- Communicate through everyday activities to help children embrace their language and learning.
- Use language and actions which show children that their views, feelings and opinions are listened to with care and attention.
- Let every child feel that he or she belongs.

EGM **Direct Observation**

NVQ 205 3 6 8

NVQ 206 K2D103 K2D104

NVQ 206 K2D103

NVQ 202 1 1

NVQ 205 3 7

NVQ 201 3 3

NVQ 206 5 5

NVQ 206 1 1 4

NVQ 201 3 2

You are now ready to move to the next chapter of your learning journey, but remember the environment *must* encourage children:

- to be creative
- to explore and investigate.

NVQ 205 2
3
5

Safe environments

You will learn how to prepare and maintain the physical environment to a safe and healthy standard. You will also learn how to build environments that allow children to take part in drama and imaginative play, thereby building their confidence and supporting their language and communication development.

NVQ 205 1
NVQ 202 1
NVQ 206 2
NVQ 205 3
NVQ 206 1

As you work with children during the next few weeks, you will learn how different environments can support various activities and promote developmental growth. First, let's look at a safe physical environment.

Hints & Tips

Don't forget that the environment includes both indoor and outdoor settings.

Basic rules will apply whichever environment you are creating:

- Be effective with your use of space. (NVQ 205 1 1)
- Set out the furniture and equipment to allow children and adults ease of movement. (NVQ 205 1 2)
- Always keep exits and entrances free of furniture and equipment. (NVQ 205 1 3)
- Ensure the environment complies with health and safety requirements. (NVQ 205 2 7)

Whenever possible, let the children help you with arranging the environment.

NVQ 205 1 5

Make sure the environment is suited to the children's needs and abilities, and that it can be adapted and changed as required.

NVQ 205 1 6, 8; 2 8, 9

Ensure that health and safety policies and procedures that apply to the environment are upheld within your setting.

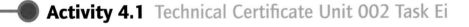

NVQ 205 K2H65

Activity 4.1 Technical Certificate Unit 002 Task Ei

T.Cert 002 Task E i

A safe environment should meet the needs of children.

Plan a room to meet children's and young people's physical, social, emotional, language and intellectual needs, taking into acount their age, gender, culture, ethnicity, needs and abilities. Give reasons for the key features of your plan.

NVQ 205 K2D59 K2D60

Show the position of furniture, equipment, learning areas and other items.

Mark the position of the doors, windows and fire exits.

EGM Assignment
EGM Work Product

NVQ 205 1 3

- Mark in the learning areas necessary for the framework/curriculum of your setting.
- Explain how the layout encourages children to take part in activities.

TARGET DATE:

Activity 4.2 Questions 47–50

Q47) How can children help set up the environment?

NVQ 205 K2D61
NVQ 205 1 5

Q48) State how the environment can be adjusted as the needs of the children alter.

NVQ 205 K2D68
NVQ 205 1 6

Q49) Say how the environment meets the needs of the children in your setting, including those with disabilities and special educational needs.

NVQ 205 K2D70

Q50) State how you have met the principles and values of the sector.

Principles and Values

TARGET DATE:

Activity 4.3 Technical Certificate Unit 002 Task Avi

T.Cert 002 Task A vi

Give a brief description of the emergency procedures for:

- fire
- security incidents
- missing children/young people.

NVQ 202 K2H30

EGM Assignment

TARGET DATE:

Healthy environments

Activity 4.4 Questions 51–58

EGM Questioning

Before you move on to actually setting up the different environments for the children, carry out some personal research to find out the ideal requirements for a (safe and) healthy environment. Answer these questions and include this as evidence in your portfolio.

Q51) What is the recommended temperature for a childcare setting? — NVQ 205 1 7

Q52) Why and how is the setting ventilated? — NVQ 205 K2H73

Q53) How can you ensure a setting is accessible to all children and their carers? — NVQ 205 1 8

Q54) How do you deal with waste safely, according to the procedures of the setting? — NVQ 202 1 4; NVQ 202 K2H20; NVQ 208 K2H139

Q55) Record good hygiene practices within the childcare setting. — NVQ 202 K2H24

Q56) How do you attempt to avoid cross-infection? — NVQ 202 K2H24

Q57) What are the health and safety regulations for handling body fluids? — NVQ 202 K2H24

Q58) What is the policy in your setting for preventing the spread of HIV and hepatitis? — NVQ 202 K2H24

TARGET DATE:

Continue to research or ask colleagues for information on the following two important health and safety issues. — NVQ 204 2 1

Activity 4.5 Questions 59–60

EGM Questioning

Q59) What are the regulations in your setting covering manual handling and the risks associated with lifting and carrying children? — NVQ 202 K2P18 2

Q60) Describe the organisation's practices regarding risk assessment and safety. — NVQ 208 K2H124

TARGET DATE:

All those involved with children and young people need to ensure that they plan and create an environment that is caring, stimulating and safe. Resources and equipment must be suitable and possible risks identified and minimised wherever possible. — Common Core 3; Outcomes Framework 2

Activity 4.6 Technical Certificate Unit 002 Task Ai

T.Cert 002 Task A i

NVQ 202 K2S15

NVQ 202 K2H16

EGM Assignment

TARGET DATE:

List and briefly describe two of the main pieces of health and safety legislation that promote safe working practices in a childcare environment (relevant to the country in which you are working).

Activity 4.7 Technical Certificate Unit 002 Task Aii

T.Cert 002 Task A ii

NVQ 205 1 4
NVQ 202 K2H19
K2H23

EGM Assignment

TARGET DATE:

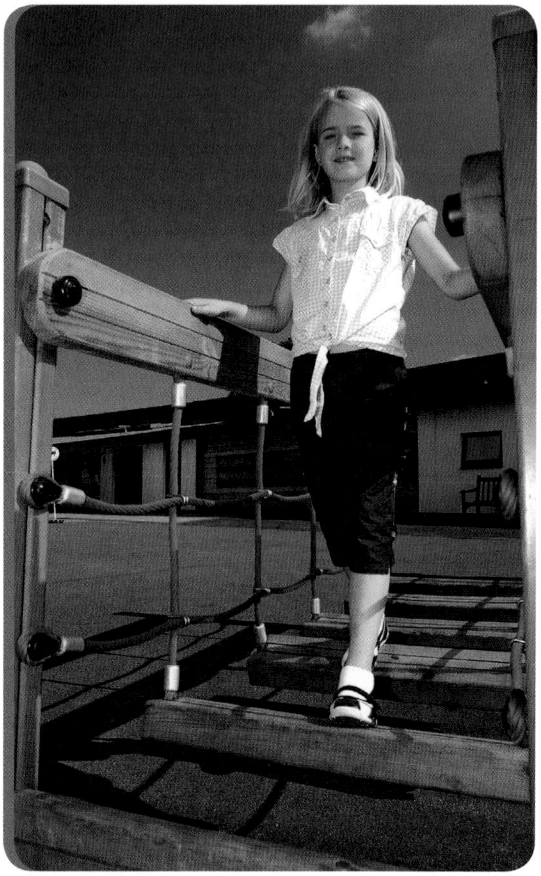

Using templates T07.1–T07.3, give two examples of the different risks and hazards that can be present in a childcare environment. Give a brief description of what can be done and which safety equipment can be used to minimise each of the risks identified.

Assignment 002 Supporting the provision of safe and effective childcare environments

T07.1

Task Aii

	AREA	RISK	HAZARD	PREVENTATIVE ACTIONS AND EQUIPMENT
	Example: Kitchen	*Burns and scalds*	*Unguarded cooker*	*Use a cooker guard* *Supervise at all times*
1	Kitchen			
2				
1	Hallway/Stairs			
2				

T07.2

	AREA	RISK	HAZARD	PREVENTATIVE ACTIONS AND EQUIPMENT
1	Bathroom/Toilet			
2				
1	Garden			
2				

T07.3

	AREA	RISK	HAZARD	PREVENTATIVE ACTIONS AND EQUIPMENT
1	Indoor play			
2				

Safety in a childcare setting must be checked at the start of the day, during the day and at the close of the day.

NVQ 202 1 2

You must maintain a safe layout and good organisation of rooms, equipment, materials and outdoor spaces.

NVQ 202 K2H21

Safety and security procedures must be implemented throughout the day for the protection of all children.

NVQ 202 1 8

Activity 4.8 Safety and security procedures

Ask if you can work alongside a colleague who will be opening the childcare setting at the beginning of the day.

NVQ 202 1 2
NVQ 202 K2H20
K2H21

Write a report on how you checked the environment (indoors and outdoors), equipment and materials to ensure safety, security and hygiene.

EGM Work Product
NVQ 202 K2S15

On a different day, ask to work the late shift so that you can assist with safety and security procedures at the end of the day.

NVQ 202 1 8

Now that you are becoming aware of safety in the environment, are recognising potential hazards and know how to deal with them, you're nearly ready to set up environments that encourage children to investigate. But first...

NVQ 202 3

NVQ 206 5

Design a template to allow staff to record toys and equipment that require attention or maintenance.

Now you need to conduct a risk assessment.

EGM Risk Assessment

TARGET DATE:

Environments to stimulate the five senses

Activity 4.9 Environment for the five senses – personal learning

Children explore and investigate through curiosity using their five senses.

It is important that you provide an environment that stimulates the five senses, promotes problem solving, recall and extended thinking, and yet sets out practical daily activities and works within the routines of the setting to support play and learning.

NVQ 206 K2D106
K2D107
K2D110

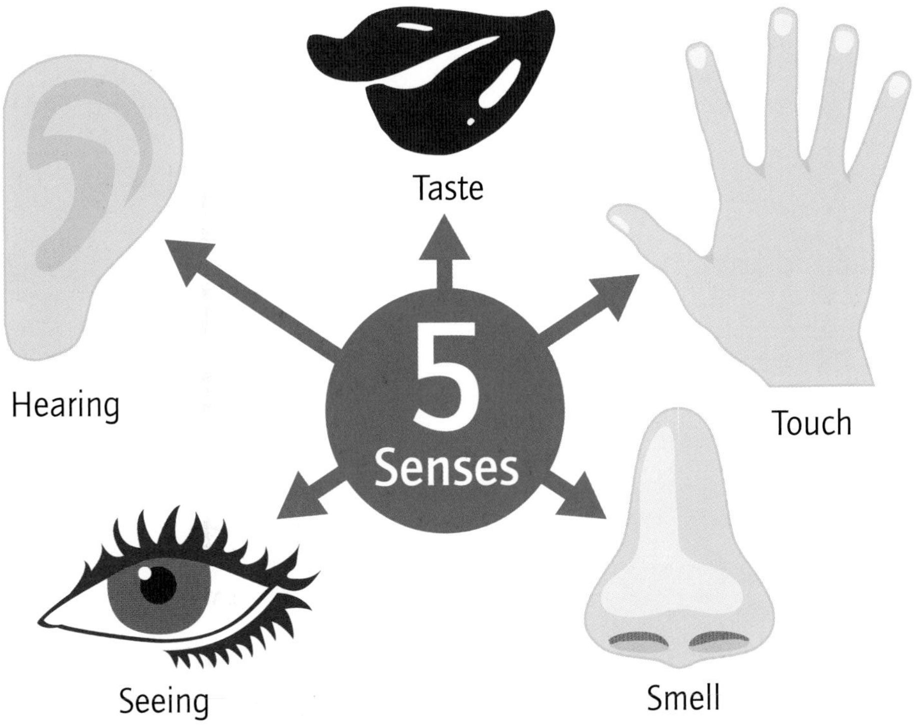

Carry out some personal learning on the development of the five senses and how you can contribute to children's development.

Use your new knowledge and skills to improve your practice.

NVQ 204 2 4

TARGET DATE:

Activity 4.10 Environment for the five senses – action plan

EGM Action Plan

NVQ 205 2 2, 4, 5, 6

With the use of an action plan, list the activities you will set out in the indoor/outdoor environment to promote the development of the five senses. Use different colours to make the environment interesting and exciting.

NVQ 205 2 1, 3

When setting up this environment with the help of the children, use visual and tactile displays that promote positive images of people in line with the principles and values of the sector.

In your own words, describe how vibrant and exciting your environment looked.

EGM Work Product

TARGET DATE:

Activity 4.11 Questions 61–62

NVQ 205 2 7

NVQ 205 K2D75

Q61) What health and safety issues did you consider?

Q62) Why are consistent routines important to the child within a changing environment?

NVQ 205 2 6

EGM Direct Observation

EGM Questioning

When you have planned the set-up of the environment to stimulate the five senses, make an appointment with your assessor to observe.

Activity 4.12 Narrative on stimulation

NVQ 205 K2D66

Record how you stimulated each of the senses and the effects of the stimulation, along with the children's reactions.

TARGET DATE:

Activity 4.13 Tape recording

EGM Witness Testimony

NVQ 205 2 5

NVQ 206 K2D90

Make a tape recording of the children as you sing and make music and sounds. Play the tape back to the children and record their comments for evidence (and communication).

EGM Tape Recording

TARGET DATE:

Environments for investigation

Activity 4.14 Environment for investigation

Working within the framework or curriculum theme of your setting, plan, prepare and set up a safe and healthy environment that encourages children, using a variety of activities and materials they can explore and investigate.

NVQ 206 K2D88
NVQ 202 1
NVQ 206 5

This can be an exciting environment to set up, as you can prepare and display objects from different cultures and from your local community, for the children to examine.

NVQ 206 5 1 3
NVQ 206 K2D105 K2D98
NVQ 205 K2D70
NVQ 202 K2D38

Alternatively, you could set up an environment that displays all the common aspects of your framework curriculum theme. For example, if your theme is farm animals, set up display areas that are related to farms and animals, e.g. a field with tractors and harvesters, a tray of dirt for sowing seeds, water with hoses for washing animals and their homes, pigsties, chickens, horses and stables, different types of food the animals are fed, hay, straw, trees, fields, etc.

If there is a farm in your locality, try to take the children there for an outing – it makes learning more realistic and fun.

NVQ 202 K2D38

On your return from the farm, encourage the children to participate in activities such as painting pictures of animals or using junk modelling to create visual images of what they have seen at the farm.

Be sure to display their pictures and models along with any photographs you may have taken. This all helps to acknowledge the achievements of each child.

NVQ 205 3 1
NVQ 205 K2D63

DON'T FORGET

Remember that the environment can be an indoor or outdoor setting.

NVQ 206 5 2

Always remember safety when you set up the environment with different objects. Whether it be the room, a table or a wall, young children explore by feeling, sucking and chewing, so ensure there are no loose parts and that objects are made of non-toxic materials and are too big for children to swallow.

Outcomes Framework 3

Common Core 3

Make sure your activities allow for the daily normal routines.

NVQ 205 K2D75

You should always ensure your environment allows for the developmental areas – physical, intellectual, emotional, social, language and communication – and that it is appropriate for the age, stage and needs of the children.

NVQ 206 K2D108 K2D109 K2D92

Encourage their learning by using open-ended questions, recall, prediction and extending their thinking into questions.

Inform your assessor when you are ready and prepared to carry out this activity.

EGM Direct Observation

TARGET DATE:

Activity 4.15 Questions 63–66

Q63) List the objects and artefacts you have used, with notes stating why.

EGM Questioning

Q64) Report how your environment complied with health and safety.

Q65) How did you help children to recognise their own achievements?

NVQ 205 3 3

Q66) What were the aims and objectives of your environment and were they achieved?

TARGET DATE:

Environment to encourage language and communication

Activity 4.16 Environment for language

It is time now for you to design an environment that will encourage children to gain confidence, and extend their language and communication skills through role play, drama and imaginative play.

Think about the interests and needs of each of the children before you build this environment. Is it going to be emphasising a culture or a season? Could it depict a story that the children particularly like? Remember to explain any foreseeable changes to the child's environment, providing reassurance and explanations as necessary.

NVQ 205 3 4

NVQ 205 3 5

As you design the environment, ensure you use some old familiar resources and equipment as well as the new exciting materials.

EGM Direct Observation

Provide and use a range of materials, equipment, furniture and props to support drama and imaginative play.

NVQ 206 2 1

Take part in the activities, showing your own interest in exploring and investigating. Make sure the activities chosen are suitable for the children and arouse their curiosity. Supervise their safety and support them appropriately for their age, needs and ability. Teach them to be aware of their own safety and that of others.

NVQ 206 5 4
1 6
NVQ 202 1 5
6
NVQ 206 2 6
5 6
8

Allow children to select equipment and materials that stimulate their interest and extend their knowledge of their own and others' cultures.

NVQ 206 2 2

Ensure the activities are carefully prepared, the environment is safe and child friendly, and allows them to explore and investigate freely without concern.

NVQ 206 5 6
7

In your role as childcare practitioner, you need to support, extend and promote language skills, meeting the different learning styles of the children in your group. You need to maintain their attention and encourage participation through a variety of activities that use drama and imagination.

If you take part in their imaginative play, you can extend it, encouraging and supporting them to explore their own feelings and those of others.

NVQ 206 2 4

At other times you need to allow the children to play freely without adult intervention. When requested by the children, you can be part of their imaginative play or you can add more props, where relevant.

NVQ 206 2 5
3
3 1
NVQ 206 K2D96

Encourage children to avoid stereotyping in their drama.

NVQ 206 2 3

- Use eye contact, body movement and voice effectively.

NVQ 206 1 3

- Use role play to enhance and give confidence to communication.

NVQ 206 1 5

- Use music, movement and rhythm to encourage communication.

NVQ 206 1 2

Help children to express their needs and make choices.

NVQ 201 3 3

When you have planned your activities and are ready to set up the environment, make a date for observation with your assessor.

EGM Direct Observation

After the observation, record a professional discussion with your assessor about the activities you set up within the environment, using the list you drafted previously. Discuss any alternative play activities or ideas you may have about environments.

EGM Professional Discussion

TARGET DATE:

The creative environment

The next environment you are going to set up is one that stimulates children's creativity.

Creative play promotes learning and development. It helps with children's emotional development as it allows them to express their feelings through creativity. It also helps promote intellectual development as it introduces children to a range of different colours, smells and textures.

Children's social development is encouraged as they work alongside each other, sharing ideas, materials and tools. Language development is automatically nurtured as children talk to each other and adults. Physical skills are promoted as the children cut, stick, screw, glue and paint.

NVQ 205 2
NVQ 206 3

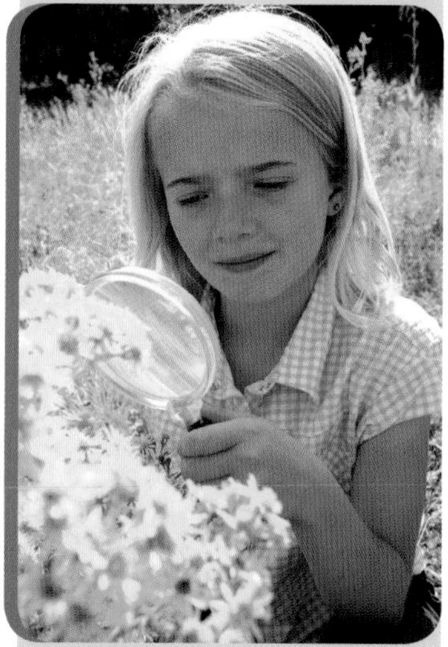

Activity 4.17 Environment for creativity

Set up an environment that will stimulate children's creativity.

NVQ 206 K2D97

EGM Expert Witness Testimony

Consider the following points:

- The environment is appropriate to the children's age and developmental stage.
  NVQ 205 2 8
  NVQ 206 3 4
- It is for indoors and outdoors.
- All aspects of the environment comply with health and safety.
  NVQ 205 2 7
  NVQ 205 K2H65
  NVQ 202 K2D22
- The environment can be adapted according to the needs of the children.
  NVQ 205 2 9
  NVQ 205 K2T67 K2D68
- Ensure that you provide a range of materials, equipment and props to support creativity and the children's interest.
  NVQ 206 3 1
- Make sure you boost and support children's confidence as they make and create things, praising their effort rather than the end product.
  NVQ 206 K2D99
- Allow children to help choose materials and ensure that your environment allows for the development of all five senses.
  NVQ 205 2 6
  NVQ 205 K2D61 K2D66

Ensure that your environment is interesting and exciting, and stimulates the children's interest with lots of brilliant, intense colours, music and sounds.

NVQ 205 2 4 5

When you are ready to set up the environment and you have activities planned that will allow for:

- sand, water and modelling clay
- painting, using a variety of tools, mediums and shaped papers
- drawing, colouring and other mark making
- printing, using a variety of methods
- music and songs
- dance and creative movement,

make a date with your assessor for direct observations.

Write a report on each of the creations made or carried out by the children. Were your aims and objectives for each child achieved? State how.

NVQ 206 3 2

NVQ 206 3 3

EGM Direct Observation

TARGET DATE:

Activity 4.18 Technical Certificate Unit 002 Task Eii

T.Cert 002 E ii

As you have been carrying out creative activities, now would be an appropriate time to complete a Technical Certificate. Read the following scenario then carry out the task.

Harry is three years old. He has been shouting and running around, arguing with everyone. You know he has been ill and has been away from your setting for several days. He has spilt some paints, a picture he has painted is on the floor, and he has torn another child's picture.

Describe how you could use the policies and procedures of your childcare setting to respond to his range of behaviours.

NVQ 202 K2D35 K2D36 K2D37

EGM Technical Certificate
EGM Assignment

TARGET DATE:

Environmental displays

Activity 4.19 Environmental displays

Whilst you are working with children, especially in creative activities, you will be involved with helping to display their work. This should be done in ways that encourage and suppport their confidence and self-esteem, promoting positive images of people according to the values and principles of the childcare sector.

NVQ	206 3	5
NVQ	205 2	5
NVQ	205 K2D62 K2D64 K2D72 K2D74	

With the help of the children, prepare a display that is both visual and tactile, using items made from the previous activities.

NVQ	205 2	1 2

Gain an expert witness testimony and write an account of how you and the children have displayed all the work.

EGM	Expert Witness Testimony
EGM	Reflective Account

TARGET DATE:

Now that you have practised setting up some environments, carry out these written assignments.

Activity 4.20 Technical Certificate Unit 004 Task Aiii

T.Cert 004 A iii

Give a brief description of how you would plan and prepare the play and learning environment, taking into account the children's differing needs and abilities.

TARGET DATE:

Activity 4.21 Technical Certificate Unit 004 Task Aiv

T.Cert 004 A iv

Make a list of what you need to do to ensure that the environment, materials and equipment are safe and maintained appropriately.

TARGET DATE:

Activity 4.22 Technical Certificate Unit 004 Task Av

T.Cert 004 A v

Describe how to carry out a risk assessment for water play, and how risks can vary according to age, needs, ability and the environment.

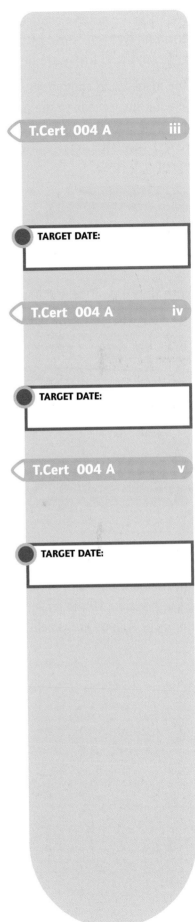

TARGET DATE:

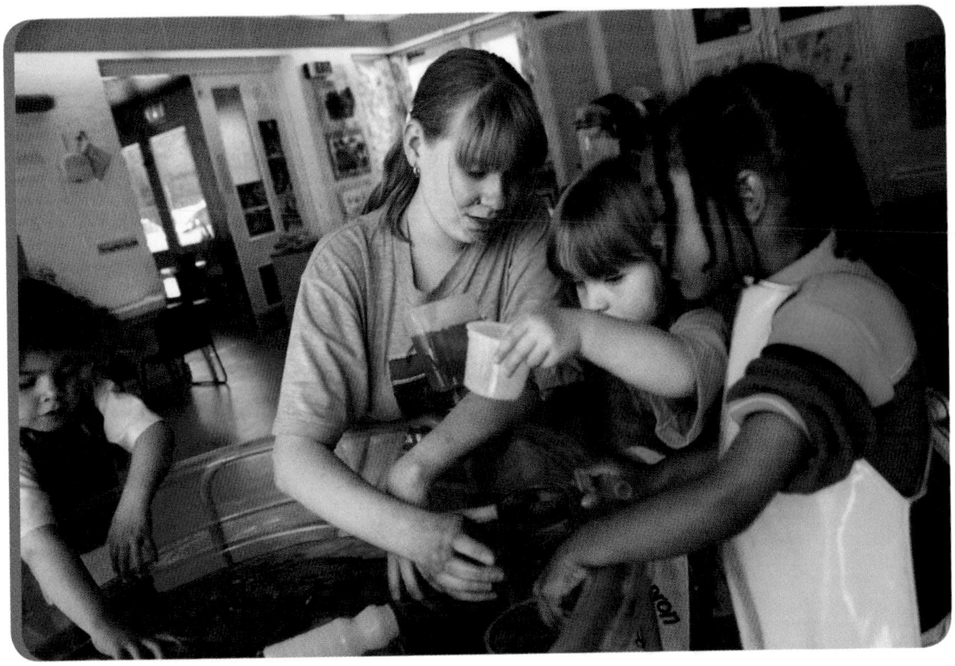

Well done! You have completed Chapter 4. Think back over all the environments you have set up. How many more could you set up? How different could they have been?

The ideas could come from the children or from your own experience of a walk in your lunch break to the nearest shopping centre! Name the shops – they could be role-play areas: chemist, florist, garage, café, library, hairdresser, grocer, greengrocers. The list is endless.

Your environment could be dedicated to a theme – seasons, colours, numbers, animals, families, countries, cultures. There are many ways to set up an environment but, with all you have learnt and the experiences you have gained, you know the environment should be rich in colours, textures, words, numbers, sounds and smells, and emulate a happy, vibrant atmosphere.

5

Babies and children aged 0–3 years

Chapter contents

Index to activities in Chapter 5

Birth to Three Matters framework

This chapter of the workbook is about children under 3 years of age. It is an optional unit.

The scope of this workbook allows you to complete two different optional units: teamwork or work with under-fives.

In this chapter you are going to learn specifically about working with babies and children aged 0–3 years.

The care of a baby is quite different to the care of a toddler, and the care of a five-year-old is different again. The different care skills continue all the way through early childhood up to adolescence.

Childcare practitioners who work with children aged 0 to 3 years must realise what a responsible job they have. Along with the parents of a child, they are the first educators, and as such are privileged to be able to watch the tiny baby gradually start to become aware of self and then others; to snuggle up and form strong relationships. Forming emotional bonds and being special to someone are key features for the childcare practitioner caring for babies.

Gradually, the baby will try and communicate; pre-verbally at first and then quite vocally. After that, the baby will be curious and want to explore, learning to sit, crawl and then walk. The pride taken in a child's first steps is shared by parents, family and childcare practitioner alike.

You need to be able to observe babies and plan their next activities, to ensure the sequence of development is encouraged.

To ensure that you gain as much knowledge and practical experience as possible, this chapter is dedicated to two different age groups:

- babies under 12 months
- children aged $2\frac{1}{2}$ to 3 years.

Common Core 2

Let's work first with babies, who can be any age under 12 months. Use the knowledge you gained in Chapter 2 as a foundation on which to build further understanding and awareness of a baby's needs and development.

You can gain this extra knowledge from books, workshops, the Internet or videos, but it is essential that, as a childcare practitioner, you try to update your knowledge frequently through your personal programme of continuous professional development.

NVQ 208 K207H10

Ask your colleagues or line manager where you could gain further personal development on a topic that would add to your knowledge of childcare.

NVQ 204 1 5

Activity 5.1 Birth to Three Matters

One topic you must understand when you are working with children aged 0–3-years is the Birth to Three Matters framework, which has been designed to help practitioners support children in their early years.

Carry out some personal research on Birth to Three Matters. Give yourself a target date for when you hope to complete your research.

NVQ 208 K2P111

NVQ 208 K2D116
NVQ 204 K2P56

EGM Personal Research

TARGET DATE:

Now that you have more knowledge about babies under 12 months of age and an understanding of the Birth to Three Matters framework, you can start to plan activities for babies using the framework, cross-referencing to each of the four components.

As a childcare practitioner, you must recognise individuals, their efforts and achievements. This can be done by careful observation.

Hints & Tips

In a moment, we'll move on to some activities, but first you need to remember to:

- forma close bond with the babies you work with
- ensureall personal care routines are enjoyable, both for you and the baby
- useall opportunities to encourage learning, language and development
- alwayshandle babies correctly, being aware of their immature cells

NVQ 208 2 1

NVQ 208 2 1

NVQ 208 2 1

- maintaina daily routine, which gives security
- givebabies time to explore their environment safely
- neverleave babies alone and be sure that they are kept safe and secure at all times.

NVQ 208 2 1
NVQ 208 K2D122
NVQ 208 2 9

TARGET DATE:

Activity 5.2 Observations on babies – personal activities

Common Core 2

Outcomes Framework 1,2

The next activity involves observing how babies move and what they can do with their body during a series of activities.

NVQ 208 1 1

Make observation notes at each activity.

EGM Child Observation

Don't forget to ask permission according to the policies and procedures of the setting.

NVQ 208 K2D114

Either ask for an expert witness testimony or make a date with your assessor.

EGM Direct Observation
EGM Expert Witness Testimony

Using equipment that has been sterilised according to the manufacturer's instructions, make up formula feeds and store them according to the procedures of the setting.

NVQ 208 2 2
NVQ 208 K2H131 K2H132

Bottle-feed each baby according to the parent's wishes and the needs of the baby.

NVQ 208 2 3
NVQ 208 K2H132

Q67) Describe how you would store expressed breast milk safely.

NVQ 208 K2H133

EGM Direct Observation

Ask a colleague to feed a baby and observe all movements. Include the winding of the baby.

NVQ 208 1 1

Q68) Write out the methods used for weaning babies. State the foods that can be given and why.

NVQ 208 K2H134

Q69) At what age does weaning generally start?

NVQ 208 K2H134

If there are babies in your group who are weaning, help them with feeding, encouraging them to enjoy their meal times.

NVQ 208 2 4

Observe a colleague feeding a baby who is being weaned.

NVQ 208 1 1
EGM Observation Notes

Wash, dress and change babies according to the procedures of the setting, using appropriate toiletries and being sensitive to the babies' needs.

NVQ 208 2 6 7

Use strict hygiene procedures and personal protection clothing as per the guidelines of the setting.

NVQ 208 2 6 7
NVQ 208 K2H138

Carry out an observation on washing and dressing the baby (not nappy changing)

NVQ 208 1 1

Q70) How do you recognise signs of distress in babies? How would you respond according to the policies and procedures of the setting?

NVQ 208 1 1, 2 5, 10

Q71) Record physical signs of illness in babies. What are the procedures for ill babies in your setting?

NVQ 208 2 5

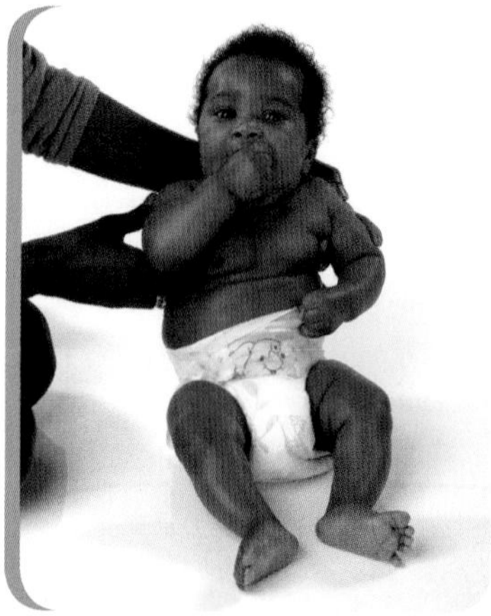

You have now observed one, two or three babies under 12 months of age.

Q72) What have you learnt from these observations about their developmental areas?

Q73) Which areas of development do you think need extra support or attention?

Share what you have observed with colleagues (and parents), according to the procedures of the setting.

NVQ 208 1 5

Now is an appropriate time for you to complete a Technical Certificate assignment.

TARGET DATE:

Activity 5.3 Technical Certificate Unit 002 Task Bi

T.Cert 002 B i

Common Core 2, 3

Outcomes Framework 1,2

EGM Expert Witness Testimony

You have been asked to plan and prepare for the care, health and safety of babies and children under 3 years of age.

Briefly describe what you need to consider when undertaking the following routine activities with a child in the age group specified.

Routine activities	Approximate age
Washing and cleansing	0–6 months
Nappy changing	6–12 months
Dressing	2–3 years
Feeding	6–18 months
Providing for sleep	2–3 years

DON'T FORGET

Each unit has a list of knowledge specifications relevant to its elements. Competent performance is dependent upon you demonstrating the knowledge through the activity.

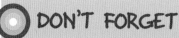

Q74) How do you care for a baby's skin when out in the sun?

NVQ 205 K2H83

TARGET DATE:

Activity 5.4 Care of hair, skin, teeth

During personal attention time, care for the hair, skin and teeth of baby according to the procedures of the setting and the needs of the baby's culture.

Dispose safely of any waste.

NVQ 208 2 8

EGM Direct Observation

NVQ 208 K2H139

EGM Expert Witness Testimony

TARGET DATE:

Activity 5.5 Technical Certificate Unit 002 Tasks Bii, Biii, Biv

T.Cert 002 B ii, iii, iv

Outline basic personal care routines for each of the following age groups:

T.Cert 002 B ii

a) 3–7 years

b) 7–12 years

c) 12–16 years.

NVQ 205 4 2 3

State how these routine activities benefit children and young people.

T.Cert 002 B iii

Common Core 2

How might you adapt these routines to meet individual needs and abilities?

T.Cert 002 B iv

Outcomes Framework 1,2

TARGET DATE:

Activity 5.6 More observations

You need to carry out some more observations on babies. The focus of your observations should be:

- how they express their feelings
- how they play (together) and have fun
- how they communicate with each other and adults.

NVQ 208 1 3

NVQ 208 1 4

NVQ 208 1 2

DON'T FORGET

Each unit has a list of knowledge specifications relevant to its elements. Competent performance is dependent upon you demonstrating the knowledge through the activity.

Let's try to observe these three skills together. (If you don't feel confident enough to do this, observe them separately.) Use an action plan to devise a range of play activities that are in line with the plans of the setting, ensuring they are suited to the abilities and needs of the babies, inclusive for all, and value diversity within the group.

NVQ 208 3 3 4 5 7
NVQ 208 K2D121 K2D125

EGM Action Plan

Ensure the activities are challenging but achievable for the babies.

NVQ 208 3 7

When you have set up your environment with the activities, complete a risk assessment stating how you minimised any hazards.

NVQ 208 K2H123 K2H124

Ask for the support of a colleague to enable you to a carry out the observation(s). Book time with your assessor and carry out the observation.

NVQ 208 3 9

Remember to give praise and support to the babies, whether they are successful or unsuccessful with their challenges.

NVQ 208 K2D126

Once you have completed the observations and are able to concentrate on playing with the babies, make sure that you:

EGM Child Observations

- use a variety of communication techniques (songs, rhymes, stories, finger and hand movements, gestures, facial expressions)

NVQ 208 4 3 6

- recognise and reward the communication efforts of babies in a way that encourages language development and positive relationships

NVQ 208 4 2

- understand the pre-verbal communication signs, supporting their efforts to verbalise

NVQ 208 K2C127 K2C128
NVQ 208 4 4

- help babies choose creative and imaginative activities that meet their identified needs

NVQ 208 3 6

- play alongside and with the babies, enjoying their company and identifying their needs from their communication, with high expectations of what they can achieve

NVQ 208 3 8
4 5

- monitor and record the responses of babies to different activities.

NVQ 208 3 9

Should you have any concerns about the development of the babies, follow the policies of the setting and report them immediately.

NVQ 208 K2D117

Record the safety policy of the setting for babies.

NVQ 208 3 2

TARGET DATE:

Activity 5.7 Questions 75–79

Q75) When a baby or child separates from its parents, record what you think are the anxieties experienced by the:

- baby
- child
- parent.

NVQ 208 4 1
NVQ 208 K2T130

Q76) How would you give support?

Q77) If a baby was new to the setting, how would you help him or her to settle in and try to reduce the anxieties of the parent(s)?

NVQ 205 4 1

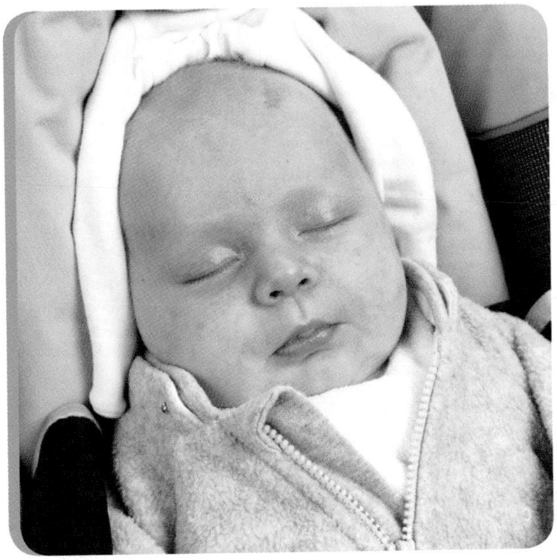

Q78) How did you use the Birth to Three Matters framework to help you set up your activities?

NVQ 208 K2D116

Q79) Record the difference between formal and informal observations, giving examples of each.

NVQ 208 K2D112

Early Years Foundation

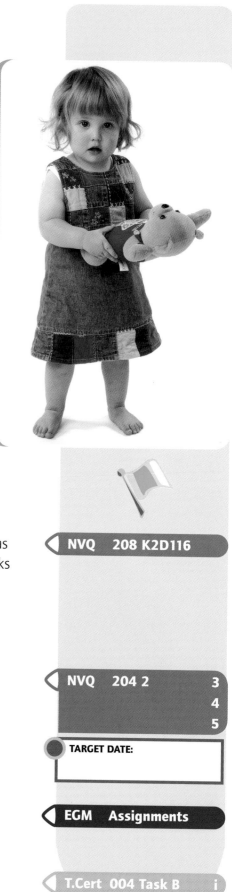

It is time now to move on to the more complex growth and development of the toddler and child. This is a fascinating journey.

From the small, relatively helpless baby that you have been observing and supporting emerges the toddler, curious and keen to look at and try all sorts of activities, whether dangerous or not. The child has learnt many skills – sitting, crawling, walking, talking, playing and pretending – but still has to mature and perfect these skills to be ready for the new world of investigating, sharing, competing, discussing, problem solving, demonstrating and, finally, taking on responsibilities.

Again, you must be conversant with the Birth to Three matters framework, which aims towards each child becoming a strong child, a healthy child, a skillful communicator and a competent learner.

Once the three-year-old has mastered the skills outlined in the Birth to Three Matters framework, and knows how to form relationships with peer group and adults, he or she will be ready to start learning through the structured framework of the Early Years Foundation.

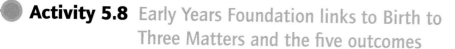

Activity 5.8 Early Years Foundation links to Birth to Three Matters and the five outcomes

NVQ 208 K2D116

For your first activity with the nearly-three-year-old, read through the six areas of the Early Years Foundation and note down how Birth to Three Matters links to the Early Years Foundation and, briefly, how each of them maps to the components of the five outcomes from Every Child Matters.

This knowledge will help you create progressively harder activities for the support and promotion of the developing child.

Speak to your assessor and clarify any points you are unsure about.

NVQ 204 2 3 4 5

TARGET DATE:

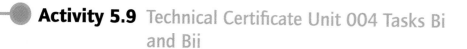

Activity 5.9 Technical Certificate Unit 004 Tasks Bi and Bii

EGM Assignments

Briefly outline the content and purpose of an early education curriculum framework.

T.Cert 004 Task B i

Look at the answers you gave in Task Aii Unit 004 (Activity 1.10), where you identified different play activities. Take each activity and outline how it relates to the formal curriculum frameworks in the country in which you are working.

T.Cert 004 Task B ii
NVQ 206 K2D88
K2D116

TARGET DATE:

Activity 5.10 New child

When you know that you have a new child starting in your centre, ask your line manager if you could help with settling in the child.

EGM Action Plan

Following the routine procedures of the setting, prepare an action plan that clearly states the measures you will take for the preparation of settling a new child into your group.

NVQ 205 4 1
NVQ 205 K2D69
K2D70
K2D71

You must consider the needs of the child, the family and the rest of the child's peers in the group.

EGM Eye Witness Testimony

When you feel confident, set out a range of activities for your group of children, both indoors and outdoors, that will support different aspects of learning and development and encourage them to include and play with each other. Be sure you have activities that will be appropriate for the new child.

NVQ 208 3 1
3
4
5
6
7

EGM Direct Observation
EGM Expert Witness Testimony

Carry out a risk assessment to ensure safety is being followed and hazards are minimised.

NVQ 208 3 2
EGM Risk Assessment

TARGET DATE:

Activity 5.11 New child settling in

When you are ready for assessment, inform your assessor of the date and time.

Working within the routines of the setting, help to settle the new child into your group.

Ensure you have the following in place:

- consistent routines that allow for quiet play and physical play, both indoors and outdoors
- personal care routines that are enjoyable experiences and are used to develop relationships and encourage language and learning
- procedures to comfort children when they are distressed, according to their needs
- systems which ensure children are never alone and are kept safe and secure at all times.

Write a report for your line manager, recording how the child settled into the setting. Are there any tasks you would do differently next time?

NVQ 205 4 1

EGM Direct Observation

NVQ 205 3 2

NVQ 205 4 3
2 1

NVQ 208 2 10

NVQ 208 2 9

EGM Report

TARGET DATE:

Activity 5.12 New child playing

Ask a colleague for support to enable you to observe the children in different activities.

When you have introduced the new child to his or her peer group and they are all playing on activities indoors and out, observe how the children move round the activities. Note what they can do with their body and how they use both gross and fine motor muscles.

NVQ 208 1 1

EGM Group Observation

TARGET DATE:

Activity 5.13 Professional discussion

Carry out a professional discussion with your assessor, reporting why you set out the activities in Activity 5.10, the skills you used in settling in the new child and the value of your observation. Discuss with your assessor how you will set out your next set of activities, indoors and out, giving reasons why.

NVQ 204 1 3

EGM Professional Discussion

TARGET DATE:

Activity 5.14 Play

Set out a range of activities that will support different areas of play, ensuring that you include:

- activities that will promote communication
- activities that will promote play.

NVQ 208 1 2

Inform your assessor when you are ready for assessment.

EGM Direct Observation

Make notes or complete checklists whilst you observe children communicating with adults and peers. Observe how they express their feelings, noting how they play alone and in groups.

Whilst the children are playing and you make notes, you must also show children the following considerations:

- Pay attention to the children and listen, asking questions to confirm and show your understanding of their language, and helping them to express their needs and make choices.

NVQ 201 1 1
6
3 3

- Demonstrate your understanding of children's preferred ways of communicating by acknowledging their efforts at expression and their show of feelings.

NVQ 201 1 4
5
3 2
4
NVQ 208 3 9

- Monitor and record their responses to different activities.
- Use your own positive communication skills for the children, encouraging them to use a variety of communication methods.

NVQ 201 1 5
6
NVQ 208 4 6

- Use a sympathetic approach whilst listening to children, playing alongside them, encouraging their achievements and enjoying their company.

NVQ 201 1 2
NVQ 201 K2C1
NVQ 208 3 8

TARGET DATE:

Activity 5.15 Records

You have now carried out activities and observations for both babies and children. You need to share what you have observed with the appropriate people, according to the procedures of the setting.

Record information on babies' and children's progress and areas of development that require further support (according to the policy and procedures of the setting).

NVQ 208 1 5

NVQ 208 1 6

TARGET DATE:

Activity 5.16 Questions 80–82

Q80) If a baby is sleeping during the day in a childcare setting in his or her own cot, what are the current safety procedures to protect the child from SIDS (Sudden Infant Death Syndrome)?

Q81) You have been asked by a $2\frac{1}{2}$-year-old's mum to help her child with toilet training. How would you carry this out?

Q82) If a child or a child's parents were deaf, they would communicate via a type of sign language. This might be British Sign Language or Makaton. Why is it important to use and recognise language formats?

NVQ 208 K2H141

NVQ 208 K2D140

NVQ 208 K2C129
NVQ 208 4 7

TARGET DATE:

Excellent – another chapter completed. Just one more to go!

As you have worked through the questions and activities in this book, you will have noted there has been some repetition. You would be wise to check your tracking with your assessor before completing the last chapter – it might save you time.

Good luck!

Support for all

6

Chapter contents

Index to activities in Chapter 6

As you reach the final chapter of your journey through the apprentice's framework of qualifications, we must draw together those skills, competences and knowledge that you have not yet learnt or practised.

To gain the Level 2 NVQ in Children's Care, Learning and Development, you need to complete the six mandatory units and one optional unit.

This assessment book is primarily for apprentices who wish to work with children aged 0–3 years, but every successful practitioner working in a quality childcare setting needs the support of colleagues and the flexibility and responsiveness of a team to contribute to themselves being competent.

This means, as was said at the beginning of your journey, that you will be completing two optional units instead of just one. Speak to your assessor to confirm the authority to do this.

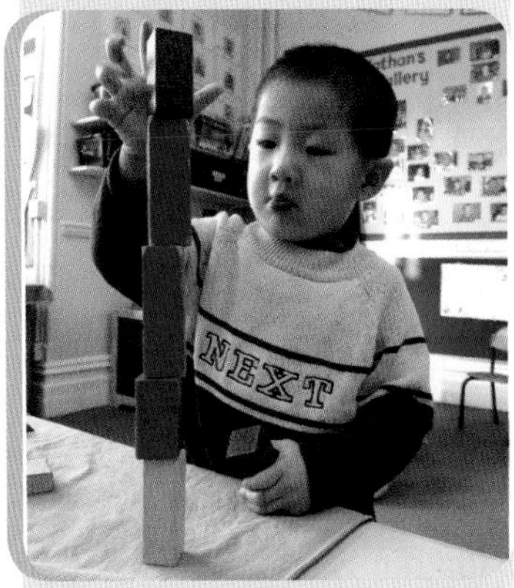

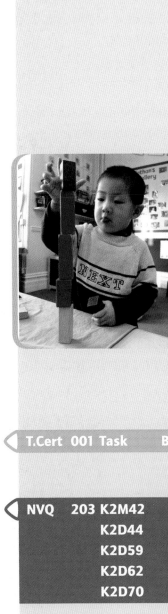

Hopefully by now you have become an important member of the team, one who is trusted, respected and allowed to care for the personal needs of the children according to the policies and procedures of the setting. (Remember safeguarding, and never allow yourself to be left alone with a child or children.)

You have observed how new children have been gently settled into the childcare setting and taken an active part in their security.

You have now been asked to take the lead in settling Amelie into the setting.

Activity 6.1 Technical Certificate Unit 001 Task Bii

T.Cert 001 Task Bii

Read the following case study then answer the related questions.

NVQ 203 K2M42 K2D44 K2D59 K2D62 K2D70

Amelie is a three-year-old girl from Mauritius. She has just started at your setting and her family is new to the area. All you have been told is that she comes from a lone-parent family and has dyspraxia. You have been asked to talk with Amelie's parent to help plan Amelie's care, learning and development.

1. Briefly describe how you would establish and maintain a positive relationship with Amelie and her parent.
2. What are the policies and procedures of your setting regarding sharing information and what would you need to tell Amelie's parent about confidentiality?
3. What information would you need to help plan for Amelie?
4. How can you make sure that Amelie is included and treated equally within your setting, without discrimination?

TARGET DATE:

Activity 6.2 Technical Certificate Unit 001 Task Bi

T.Cert 001 Task Bi

Britain is a diverse and inclusive society. Choose two different cultural, social or ethnic groups and describe how you would celebrate their different beliefs, traditions, customs and festivals in everyday practice within the childcare environment.

TARGET DATE:

NVQ 205 4 2

During the day in your childcare setting, you probably work in small teams, caring for the all-round needs of the children. You ensure that there is a balance of quiet times, creative times, time for singing, music and movement, time for physical play and time for eating, drinking and sleeping.

Activity 6.3 Personal care routines

EGM Logbook

NVQ 205 4 3

NVQ 205 4 4

Explain to your assessor how you support the personal care routines of the children in your room, according to the policies and procedures of your setting.

Working with your room team, provide drinks and food to the children, ensuring their nutritional needs are met within the course of the week.

EGM Direct Observation

TARGET DATE:

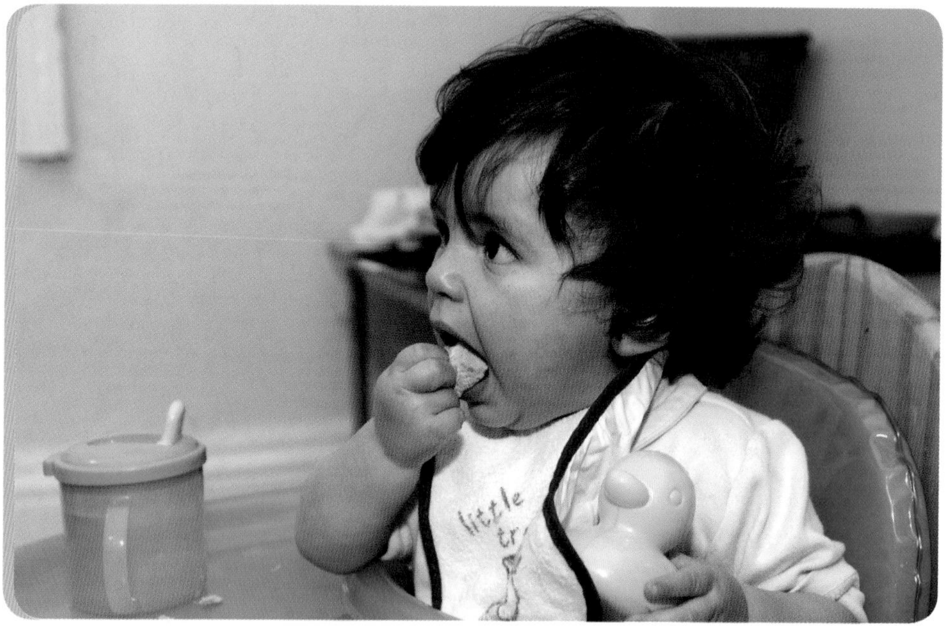

Show evidence that:

- water is available for children to drink at any time

NVQ 205 4 4

- you have completed a basic food-handling course (food handling = 2 hours; basic food hygiene = 6 hours), producing a copy of your certificate as evidence

NVQ 205 K2H78

- you follow the principles of healthy eating according to government guidelines and record them in your portfolio of evidence.

NVQ 205 K2H79

Record the allergies or sensitivities found within your group of children.

NVQ 205 K2H82

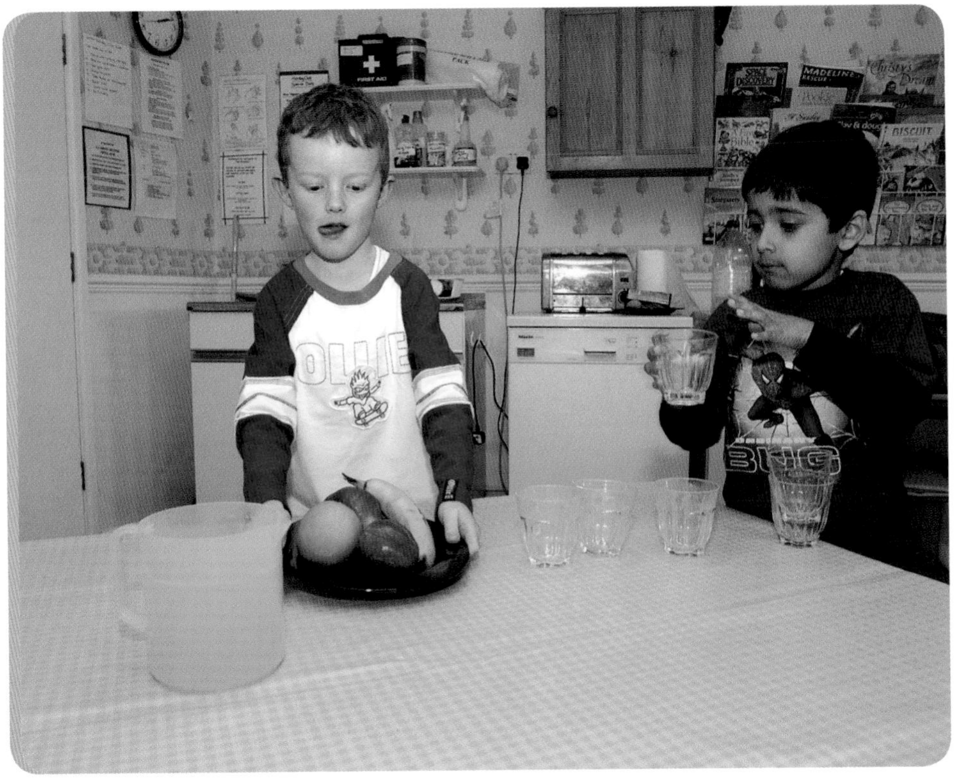

Activity 6.4 Questions 83–86

Q83) Design a chart showing the different food groups required by children and listing the nutrients found within each of the foods.

NVQ 205 K2H79
NVQ 208 K2H135

Q84) State why regular physical activity and exercise are necessary for a healthy mind and body.

NVQ 205 K2D80

Q85) Explain how you would care daily for the children's hair and skin. State which toiletries you would use.

NVQ 205 K2D83

Q86) Write down, in your own words, your understanding of 'sun safety' for children.

NVQ 205 K2D83

TARGET DATE:

Activity 6.5 Technical Certificate Unit 002 Task Ci

T.Cert 002 Task Ci

NVQ 205 K2H81

A balanced diet is essential for healthy growth and development. Produce a snack-time menu for five days for your childcare setting which provides for children or young people's nutritional requirements.

TARGET DATE:

Activity 6.6 Technical Certificate Unit 002 Task Cii

T.Cert 002 Task Cii

NVQ 205 K2H81

People have different beliefs and health needs that may affect the type of food they eat and how it is prepared. It is not possible to make full statements about all these needs but there are key principles about some of the larger groups that may be useful. Complete template T08 to show your understanding of some of these key principles.

EGM Assignments

TARGET DATE:

Activity 6.7 Technical Certificate Unit 002 Task Ciii

T.Cert 002 Task Ciii

NVQ 208 K2H139

EGM Assignments

State how you would handle food waste and body fluids in a childcare environment and why this is important.

TARGET DATE:

Assignment 002 Beliefs and health needs

T08

Task Cii

Group	One key principle
Hindu	
Muslim	
Christian	
Jewish	
Vegetarian	
Vegan	
Diabetic	
Coeliac	
Allergies/ Sensitivities	

Activity 6.8 Paediatric First Aid

NVQ 202 K2H27

If you have not attended a 12-hour paediatric First Aid course yet, speak to your assessor or tutor to book a date for this essential training. It is part of your apprenticeship framework.

EGM Paediatric First Aid

TARGET DATE:

During your time working in the childcare setting, an accident or emergency may have occurred. If this is the case, whilst the incident is fresh in your mind, recall your part in the emergency.

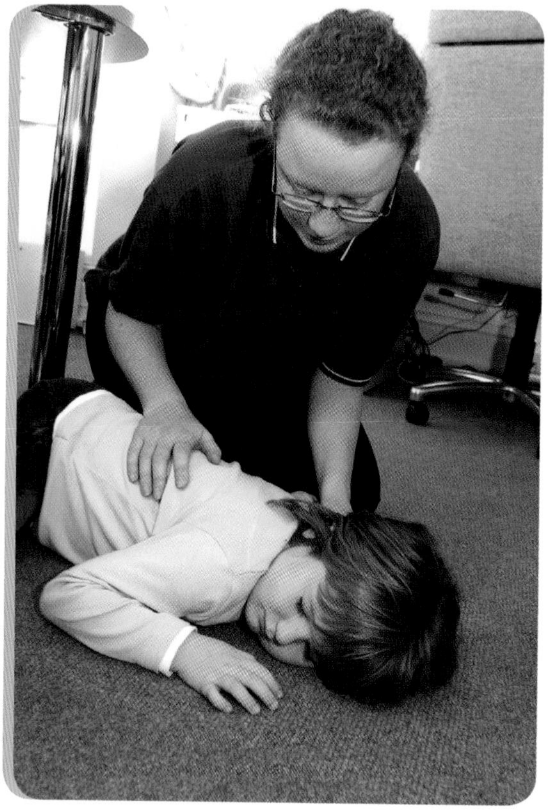

Activity 6.9 Questions 87–90

EGM Questioning

Q87) What is the procedure in your setting for accidents and emergencies? (This may be two separate procedures. Check carefully.) — NVQ 202 2 1

Q88) Who would you report to for assistance? — NVQ 202 2 2

Q89) How would you maintain the safety and security of the rest of the group and other people? — NVQ 202 2 3

Q90) How would you provide reassurance and comfort to the children and others who were involved? — NVQ 202 2 4

Write an accident report using the procedures and recording document of the setting. Ask if you can photocopy it, then remove the names and use as evidence in your portfolio. — NVQ 202 2 6

TARGET DATE:

Activity 6.10 Technical Certificate Unit 002 Task Civ

T.Cert 002 Task Civ

Not all accidents, emergencies and illnesses can be prevented. Give two common examples of each that may occur in a childcare environment.

TARGET DATE:

Accidents, emergencies and other alerts can be frightening and it is essential that you remain calm and act quickly, quietly and proficiently.

Now would be a good time to reflect back on your practice and critically analyse how you reacted and dealt with any accident or emergency.

EGM Refective Account

Activity 6.11 Technical Certificate Unit 001 Tasks Ci, Cii, Ciii

T.Cert 001 Task Ci Cii Ciii

List the different ways you can reflect on your own practice.

How will reflecting on your own practice help you to be a better childcare practitioner?

TARGET DATE:

Now is the time to think about childhood illness and children's infections. It is important that you know how to recognise when children are feeling unwell and deal with the situation appropriately.

Activity 6.12 Common illnesses

Using template T09, record common infections and illnesses that may affect children aged 0–16 years.

NVQ 208 K2H136
NVQ 202 K2H29

TARGET DATE:

Common infections/illnesses in children

T09

Infection or illness	Incubation period & isolation time	Signs and symptoms	Treatment & any complications

You are now moving on to the last set of activities for your journey through the childcare framework.

Although these activities have been left to the last chapter, it does not mean they are of less importance. In fact, the following activities and the knowledge you will learn will provide you with essential skills for dealing with children of any age.

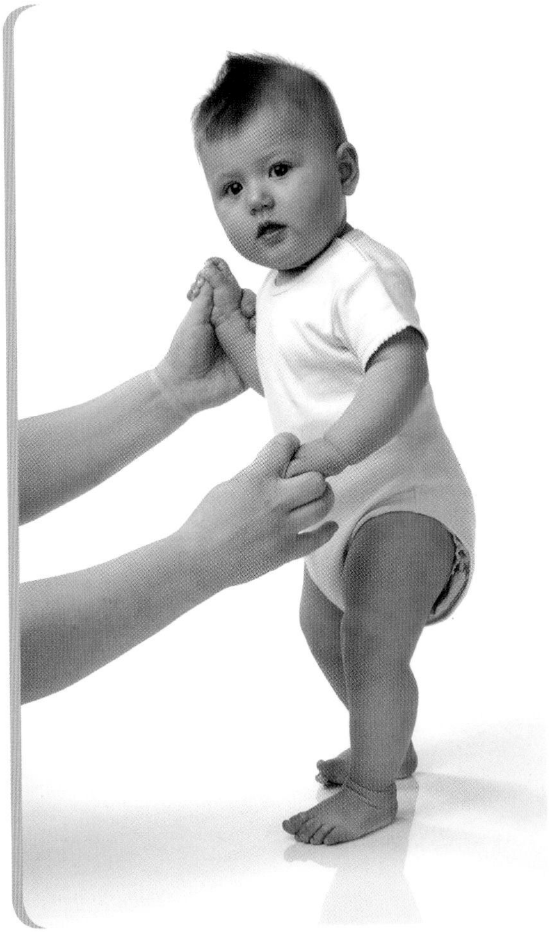

The first area of focus is the safeguarding and protecting of children. Children from all cultures, incomes and social backgrounds, irrespective of age and gender, can be the victim of any type of abuse. New government regulations demand that all people who work with children from local agencies (e.g. social services, education, police, youth service, health, probation, training and voluntary services) co-operate to protect children.

If you have any suspicion that a child is being abused or that his or her needs are being neglected, you must report this to a senior person (however hard you may find it).

NVQ 202 3 2
NVQ 202 K2S17

Activity 6.13 Technical Certificate Unit 002 Task Di

T.Cert 002 Task Di

In templates T10.1–T10.3, identify and provide a definition of each type of abuse. Then list one physical, one behavioural and one developmental indicator of possible abuse.

It is essential that you follow the policies and procedures of your setting for safeguarding and protecting children at all times. Explain to your assessor or expert witness what is meant by these policies and procedures in your setting.

NVQ 202 3 1 3
NVQ 202 K2S31

TARGET DATE:

Assignment 002 Supporting the provision of safe and effective childcare environments

T10.1

Task Di

Category	Definition	Indicator
P______________		Physical
		Behavioural
		Developmental
E______________		Physical
		Behavioural
		Developmental

T10.2

Category	Definition	Indicator
S______________		Physical
		Behavioural
		Developmental
N______/F______ to T______		Physical
		Behavioural
		Developmental

T10.3

Category	Definition	Indicator
B__________________		Physical
		Behavioural
		Developmental

Activity 6.14 Technical Certificate Unit 002 Tasks Diii, Dii, Div

Outline the main piece of legislation that relates to safeguarding children and young people, including sharing information and data protection, in the country in which you are working.

State the procedures in your organisation for sharing information if you have concerns that a child or young person is being abused.

Outline how you should respond to a child or young person who discloses to you that he or she has been abused. How would you inform him or her that you would have to share this information with others (as appropriate to the situation)?

T.Cert 002 Task Diii Dii Div

NVQ 202 K2H16 K2S33 K2S1118

EGM Assignment

NVQ 202 3 4 5

TARGET DATE:

Activity 6.15 Technical Certificate Unit 002 Task Dv

Make a resource which your childcare environment can use to help children and young people to protect themselves by building confidence and resilience.

T.Cert 002 Task Dv

NVQ 202 3 6

NVQ 202 K2S34

TARGET DATE:

Activity 6.16 Professional discussion

Your final activity is to be an in-depth professional discussion with your assessor.

The feedback the assessor gives will be structured, offering you constructive comments on your behaviour, your personal effectiveness as a team member, and your strengths and weaknesses throughout the training programme.

Prepare for this discussion by reflecting on your work as a team member.

EGM Professional Discussion

Think about your:

- behaviour and attitude
- interaction with colleagues
- communication and flexibility
- willingness to help others
- ability to accept criticism and constructive feedback.

NVQ 207 2 2, 3, 4
1 4

Also think about your personal skills of:

- maintaining confidentiality
- prioritising work schedules
- dealing with conflict.

NVQ 207 2 2, 5, 6, 7, 8, 9
NVQ 207 K207H05, K207H06, K207H07, K207H08, K207H09, K207H10

Record the professional discussion, ensuring you have evidence for all criteria of NVQ 207.2.

Ensure that you discuss:

- the value of the systems that have been made available to you for support and supervision
- the opportunities available to support you in team activities.

NVQ 204 2 3, 5
NVQ 204 K2P55

You also need to consider whether you want to advance your career in childcare. If you do, speak to your assessor about Advanced Apprenticeships (Level 3 NVQ, etc.).

TARGET DATE:

End of framework programme

You have now reached the end of your programme. You should be feeling very proud of your achievements. Childcare is not an easy option for a career. Children are demanding, tiring and, at times, frustrating; but they are also loving, kind, funny and great to be with. They deserve to be looked after properly and given the best possible chance in life. You have now learnt how this should be done.

Well done and congratulations!